WHO GETS
WHAT

WHO GETS WHAT

*Fair Compensation
after Tragedy and
Financial Upheaval*

KENNETH R. FEINBERG

PublicAffairs
New York

PublicAffairs books are available at special discounts for bulk
purchases in the US by corporations, institutions, and other
organizations. For more information, please contact the Special
Markets Department at the Perseus Books Group, 2300 Chestnut
Street, Suite 200, Philadelphia, PA 19103, call (800) 810-4145,
ext. 5000, or e-mail special.markets@perseusbooks.com.

Book Design by Brent Wilcox

The Library of Congress has cataloged the printed edition as follows:
Feinberg, Kenneth R.
    Who gets what : fair compensation after tragedy and financial
upheaval / Kenneth R. Feinberg.-1st ed.
        p.   cm.
    Includes index.
    ISBN 978-1-58648-977-9 (hardcover)
    ISBN 978-1-61039-076-7 (electronic)
    1. Damages—United States.   2. Compensation (Law)—
United States.   3. Public policy (Law)—United States.   I. Title.
KF1250.F45 2012
347.73'077—dc23

First Edition
10 9 8 7 6 5 4 3 2 1

Dedicated to the memory of my sister,
Ruth Feinberg Connors:
my greatest ally and most constructive critic.
With love and appreciation.

CONTENTS

PREFACE

This book constitutes a personal effort to summarize some of my more interesting work over the past twenty-eight years. And it has been a unique professional roller coaster filled with highs and lows. The assignments—to help design and administer various special public compensation programs—have been relatively rare; I have been called on just five times since 1984. But each assignment carries with it a highly visible and very public interest. The work is all-consuming. And it occupies an important place in American history.

Who Gets What follows in the wake of my previous effort at explaining the September 11th Victim Compensation Fund: *What Is Life Worth? The Unprecedented Effort to Compensate the Victims of 9/11* (PublicAffairs, 2005). Much has happened since then, including the benefits of historical perspective in reexamining the 9/11 fund (Chapter 3). The chapters within are designed to bring the reader up to date with my career.

All of the compensation programs raise profound public policy questions: Why were these programs created in the first place? How were they created? Are they a precedent? What have we as a people learned about the wisdom and effect of these very special programs?

At the same time, this book goes well beyond the policy implications of my public compensation determinations. I also offer personal reflections. I summarize what I have learned about human nature in compensating not only victims of tragedy but also corporate officials targeted by Congress following the 2008 financial meltdown.

The longest single chapter is devoted to the compensation program the Obama administration and BP established following the Deepwater Horizon rig explosion and oil spill in the Gulf of Mexico on April 20, 2010. But difficulties arise in retelling the story of my experiences on this assignment. The Gulf Coast Claims Facility (GCCF), established to process claims and pay cash to eligible claimants, is still operating. So I write without the benefit of historical perspective. Daily events continue to unfold, and final lessons remain to be determined. Tentative conclusions are all that can be drawn.

But focusing a chapter on the GCCF also has its advantages. As an ongoing, contemporary event still occupying media attention and some citizen interest, it is not yet part of history. This particular chapter offers my immediate reaction to day-to-day, week-to-week challenges Gulf claimants bring by demanding cash, often without any proof to back up their claims. The chapter constitutes a type of journal or diary, a primary source I hope is of value to future generations.

As I did in my approach to the 9/11 fund in *What Is Life Worth?* I again had to confront the problems and challenges of confidentiality in writing *Who Gets What*. Individual citizens who file a claim for compensation or are the subject of pay determinations pursuant to congressional directive do not anticipate that their personal information will be made public in a book. They file a claim or provide data with the expectation that all such information will remain sealed, for my eyes only. And they are correct. Confidentiality is part of the bargain in participating in these compensation programs. Accordingly, in this book I must walk the fine line between confidentiality and disclosing information of interest to the reader. Names have been changed or redacted in some cases.

I also make liberal use of composite cases to highlight a general point or summarize a series of individual submissions that represent many other claimants. Quotation marks are also used as a form of dramatic license to summarize conversations I had with various claimants and corporate officials. These conversations are based on memory; I do not claim to vouch for every word, but the thrust is accurate.

A special word of thanks to my law partner, Michael Rozen, who has assumed the unenviable task of maintaining and reinforcing contact with our various clients while I have been preoccupied with my various compensation assignments. Special praise, also, to the deputy administrator of the GCCF and my colleague for more than thirty years, Camille Biros, who helped read and edit these pages. Similarly, the final product benefited from the input and historical perspective of my brother, David, who has been at my side for more than sixty years. I also acknowledge my two valuable assistants, Susan H. Schmidt and Joyce E. DeBass Wilkins, who transcribed the entire manuscript and offered helpful suggestions. Other loyal support personnel at Feinberg Rozen LLP also contributed, as did my very thorough research assistant, Elizabeth L. Unger.

I also owe a debt of gratitude to my family, especially my wife, Dede. She has borne the brunt of my long absences and late evenings—the inevitable price of grappling with the complexities of compensation.

Finally, a particular thank-you to my editors at PublicAffairs. This is my second book published by PublicAffairs, and I continue to benefit from their wise counsel.

INTRODUCTION

In April 1984, Judge Jack B. Weinstein, sitting in federal court in Brooklyn, New York, announced that a class of 250,000 Vietnam veterans exposed to the defoliant Agent Orange while serving in Vietnam, had agreed to settle nine years of class action litigation for the then-unheard-of sum of $180 million. Six weeks earlier Weinstein had appointed me special settlement master. Around-the-clock negotiations forced me to live out of a suitcase in Brooklyn while I tried to get the veterans and the chemical industry to resolve their complex dispute. The settlement would be funded entirely by Dow Chemical, Monsanto, and the six other chemical companies that manufactured Agent Orange for the Department of Defense. The Vietnam veterans claimed that a multitude of physical injuries, illnesses, and deaths were due to their exposure to the carcinogen dioxin, the key chemical ingredient in Agent Orange. But Weinstein believed that even though the class action suit was thoroughly reasonable, no individual veteran would ultimately be able to prove that his individual injury or illness was *specifically* linked to exposure to the chemical. They would have to settle. Without a fair settlement, the veterans would never get the medical help they needed.

Though the settlement brought down the curtain on the litigation, it left crucial questions unanswered. In the absence of hard medical evidence, which Vietnam veterans would receive portions of the $180 million—and how much? On what basis would eligibility and award amounts be determined? Even with money to distribute, the question remained: Who would get what?

Pioneering a new approach unheard of in our established legal system, Weinstein decided to conduct formal court hearings around the nation, asking the veterans themselves how they would propose distributing the money. I was at his side, listening in amazement as leaders of the Vietnam veterans' community pleaded for money—not for themselves but for their brothers in arms who needed it more than they did. The battle for compensation, in this case, had evoked remarkable depths of compassion in a group of Americans who could all be considered victims. The settlement that Weinstein decided, and I administered, was a revolutionary solution to the seemingly insoluble cultural wound that the Vietnam War left in our society. We thought it would be the first—and last—time compensation would be decided outside the law in this way.

And yet years later, the 9/11 terrorist attacks once again posed this same question—who gets what? Just thirteen days after the attacks Congress enacted a law, quickly signed by President George W. Bush, establishing an unprecedented publicly funded compensation program for the families of the dead and physically injured at the World Trade Center, the Pentagon, and on the four airplanes. Under the statute, any eligible victim could voluntarily waive the right to sue in court and, instead, accept generous tax-free compensation.

I was appointed by Attorney General John Ashcroft to design, implement, and administer this unique program. During the next thirty-three months, I distributed more than $7 billion of taxpayer money to 2,880 families of the dead and 2,680 victims of the attacks who suffered various physical injuries. The new law provided me some guidance—but not much—when it came to determining eligibility to file a claim; it also afforded me wide discretion in calculating individual awards. (The average award for a 9/11 death claim turned out to be $2 million; for a physical injury claim, about $400,000.) The law required me, and me alone, to make the tough decisions.

Should a New York City policeman who safely assisted World Trade Center employees in escaping the horror by directing them to a Staten Island ferry, only to drop dead himself from a heart attack when the ferry reached its destination, be eligible for a 9/11 fund death benefit? (I concluded he was eligible.) What about a resident of Jersey City who claimed respiratory illness due to the plume of dust and debris that wafted over the Hudson River after the Twin Towers collapsed? (No, ineligible.) And who should get more—the wealthy spouse and children of a stockbroker killed in the World Trade Center or those of an immigrant working as a dishwasher in the Windows on the World restaurant? Who would get what? The answers were outside the traditions of established law and up to me to decide.

Six years later, on a beautiful fall day in October 2007, a deranged student from Virginia Polytechnic Institute and State University (Virginia Tech) methodically armed himself with various high-powered weapons and proceeded to massacre twenty-seven students and five faculty members. Reloading his weapons as he walked around the bucolic campus, he came to his end in Norris Hall, where, after ending the carnage, he took his own life. In addition to the thirty-two dead, some seventy-five students were physically injured, either by bullets or in attempting to escape the gunman. An additional three hundred students claimed various mental injuries, the result of observing the gunman from college dormitories, adjoining college buildings, and in some cases, on television.

America's charitable soul rose to the occasion. More than $7 million in unsolicited private contributions poured into the office of university president Charles Steger. Now it was Steger's turn to decide "who gets what." He asked me to help him and his senior staff in Blacksburg, Virginia, devise a compensation program for the fair, prompt distribution of the money to families we deemed eligible. But practical questions of fairness quickly arose: Should the families of the dead all receive the same compensation, or should the faculty members receive an additional amount to compensate for lost wages? How much of the $7 million should be reserved for the dead as opposed to those who were physically injured? What compensation formula could take into account the varying degrees of injury? Should a bullet wound to the chest be valued higher than a broken ankle suffered by a student jumping out of a second-floor classroom window to escape the gunman? And what about compensating students for the costs associated with purely mental anguish, such as psychiatric counseling? How would I decide who got what?

Compensation became national news in February 2009. To stem public anger at perceived Wall Street greed, Congress enacted a unique and unprecedented law in the wake of an economic meltdown. Having lent billions of taxpayer dollars to more than four hundred corporations to prevent the American economy from collapsing, the government demanded accountability. For the first time in American history, the Treasury Department would actually determine appropriate compensation for key corporate officials at the seven companies that had received the most taxpayer assistance. But who would make the case-by-case decisions? Once again, I got the call.

Appointed special master for TARP executive compensation by the secretary of the Treasury, I served as the so-called pay czar. I had the singular responsibility of evaluating and approving pay packages for the top business officials presiding over these seven companies. For sixteen months I met with corporate executives to determine who got what. And I discovered very quickly the enormous gap between Main Street thinking about corporate pay and Wall Street attitudes. Not only did the subject of corporate pay fuel heated battles in Washington (and in the elections that followed), but each compensation decision also became a symbol for some banker's or executive's self-worth. Emotional confrontations became the rule during meetings with leaders of the seven affected companies.

Then, as if one crisis weren't enough, in April 2010 the Deepwater Horizon oil rig exploded in the Gulf of Mexico, killing eleven rig workers and spewing more than 200 million gallons of oil into the Gulf. It was the largest environmental disaster in American history, triggering widespread financial uncertainty and immediate economic harm to individuals and businesses throughout the region: fishermen, shrimpers, oyster harvesters, ship captains, hotels, restaurants, and others dependent on Gulf resources for their economic livelihood.

Facing a mounting public outcry as well as direct pressure from President Barack Obama, BP agreed to create an unprecedented $20 billion escrow fund to pay all those victims killed and injured by the explosion and subsequent oil spill. But how would the money be distributed? What would an individual or business have to prove to be compensated from the fund? A fisherman who could no longer fish in Gulf waters was a relatively easy case—but what about the hotel far from the oil spill whose manager claimed a 50 percent drop in reservations due to public fears of pollution? Where to draw the line?

I was named administrator of the Gulf Coast Claims Facility (GCCF), and so it fell to me yet again to wrestle with the difficulties arising from the question of who gets what.

Throughout my career I have been called upon to try to dispense justice in a very public manner. I do not usually seek these compensation assignments, and they remain relatively rare. But when tragedy strikes and policy makers seek creative compensation solutions, I accept the call to public service.

I am often asked the obvious questions: "Why you, Ken? Why are you the person everybody turns to time and again to deal with these thorny questions? How do you parse the ethical, legal, and economic issues fairly? And how do you manage to maintain your sanity in the face of criticism and challenges to your decisions?"

In regard to the first question—why me?—I'm sure that some of it is an accident of my personal history. My work on Agent Orange led to my appointment to administer the September 11th Victim Compensation Fund; President Steger, in turn, viewed Virginia Tech as a microcosm of 9/11. My work in these matters led Treasury Secretary Timothy Geithner to get me to work on Wall Street pay. And in the wake of these tough assignments, the BP challenge followed naturally. Success breeds credibility. At the same time, I am only as successful as my last assignment.

My specialty is unique: I am a lawyer and mediator in one. When I began my work in mediation, with the Agent Orange settlement, it was a specialty that few shared. Even today my chosen legal specialty, a field known as alternative dispute resolution (ADR), is a small but growing subset of our far larger legal system. Most attorneys, well versed in the law, seek professional success and respect by focusing on litigation, corporate mergers and acquisitions, and trusts and estates, among other specialties. Yet few lawyers are called upon to do what I do.

I've learned a great deal from the challenges I've faced in my career to date—and not just about the practical details of designing and running a special compensation program. To evaluate the value of a life or a livelihood, I must first tackle a set of far bigger philosophical questions: Why should public or private money be used to compensate certain citizens while denying similar generosity to others? Why do policy makers establish unique compensation regimes that are then discarded as so many aberrations? What is the role of money in our society, the role of government in healing traumatic wounds and divisions that rip us apart, and what does this tell us about the very nature of justice itself?

Why do we automatically equate dollars with payment and worth? Other societies may define "compensation" as nonmonetary: for example, an apology, a willingness on the part of the wrongdoer to assist the victim without pay until the wrong has been righted, the transfer of personal goods from one party to another as a form of barter, or perhaps a strict liability regime where wrongs are accepted as part of human nature and private compensation of any type is ignored. In such societies the transfer of money from a wrongdoer to a victim is not a bedrock principle of "compensation."

But in our America, dating back to the founding of the Republic, monetary compensation has always been integral to our legal system. And administering justice has always depended on our courts, and the adversary system pitting lawyer against lawyer, as the best way to get at the truth and promote the right result. Alexis de Tocqueville saw this as early as 1840 when, in traveling throughout nineteenth-century America, he noted that "there is hardly a political question in the United States which does not sooner or later turn into a judicial one."

Therefore, this book focuses on an accepted given in American society: that compensation consists largely of the transfer of money from one party to another, and that when one is deemed deserving, it is the checkbook rather than other consideration that determines value. The real issues posed, beginning with Agent Orange in 1984, and continuing up to my work in administering the GCCF in 2012, are all the same: When, and under what circumstances, do we create alternative compensation mechanisms to deal with a nationally recognized tragedy? Who should be deemed eligible to receive public or private compensation in such limited circumstances? And finally, what amount of compensation is deemed appropriate? My personal experiences over the past twenty-eight years give me a unique perspective in addressing these public policy issues.

I've learned that "who gets what?" is a vital question that sheds light on many little-explored corners of human nature. In the pages that follow, I'll share some of my answers—tentative, incomplete, but worthy, I hope, of examination.

– 1 –

THE PROFESSOR,
THE JUDGE, THE LAWYER,
AND THE SENATOR

Life rarely works out as planned, for reasons that are varied and often unpredictable. A lost opportunity for professional advancement turns out to be a blessing in disguise. Illness, personal relationships, family squabbles, financial considerations, changing priorities—all lead us to the road not taken.

I never anticipated a legal career spent attempting to mend the damage wrought by public tragedies. If terrorists had not struck the World Trade Center and the Pentagon, if a deranged gunman had not fired at random at Virginia Tech, if an oil rig had not exploded in the Gulf of Mexico, if the nation had not been forced to confront the worst financial crisis since the Great Depression, I would have spent my career mediating and negotiating disputes without public scrutiny. Content with my law practice, hopefully achieving the respect and admiration of my colleagues, family, and friends, I would have sought financial success while achieving some measure of personal satisfaction in helping individuals and businesses stay out of court by resolving their differences.

Growing up in urban Brockton, Massachusetts, in the years following World War II had a profound and lasting effect on me. The son of a proud father who idolized his three children, and a nurturing mother whose family was her top priority, I became convinced early on that I could somehow, somewhere make my mark and achieve success.

Brockton was an interesting place after World War II. Living in what once was the shoe capital of the world (half the boots worn by Union soldiers during the Civil War were manufactured in Brockton), its residents remembered the success and promise of the postwar era. As uncertain as the future may have been, they clung to optimism. An ethnic mix of Italians, Irish, and a modest but vibrant Jewish population, coupled with a fair number of old-time Protestant Yankees who could trace their lineage to Revolutionary War days, the people of Brockton, including the three Feinberg children and their friends, were convinced that all life's obstacles could be overcome.

The security of our parents' love had a great deal to do with this. But there was more. Assimilation—a fervent belief that we were an integral part of modern America after World War II—was a given. And a tight-knit Jewish community (there were three synagogues in Brockton) reinforced the philosophy that hard work and individual initiative, along with community support and a communitarian ethic that recognized the need to help one another in times of trial, almost guaranteed financial success and personal happiness, especially for the up-and-coming generation.

This notion of communitarian reinforcement and obligation would forever remain part of my character and personality. Giving back to the community, helping to maintain community-wide values, promoting the idea of collective goodwill—these were the objectives that defined good citizenship. They would provide an important foundation of values that grounded my future public and private work.

And there was an additional factor that certainly influenced me. My teenage years were during the time of President John F. Kennedy, a true son of Massachusetts. I was captivated—we all were excited—by this young, vibrant new president and his beautiful wife and young family. His call to public service struck a chord with me. His exhortation that each of us do something for our country had a profound effect on this young teenager from Brockton. I would always carry the idea that serving the public interest was both noble and fulfilling. Government—good government—could help improve the lives of all Americans. I wanted to be part of the effort.

Brockton in the 1950s and 1960s shaped my character and priorities. It taught me that I controlled my destiny.

———

I attended the University of Massachusetts and did well enough to gain admission to the New York University School of Law. Law school in New York was an experience like no other. I studied law during the day; theater, opera, concerts, and socializing in Greenwich Village at night expanded my horizons and honed my intellectual curiosity and outlook. I achieved top grades and was invited to join the law review as an articles editor (a senior management position reserved for the best law students).

More important, I fell under the spell of my first real mentor. Because I had received a scholarship to ease my financial burden, the law school required me to devote ten hours a week as a research assistant, working closely with a faculty member. After a competitive interview, Professor Robert Pitofsky put me to work doing legal research in his area of expertise, federal antitrust law.

Pitofsky was an accomplished law professor; students lined up to gain admission to his classes. He was also a nationally recognized antitrust expert, the coauthor of a highly regarded textbook, and a skilled antitrust lawyer. A true renaissance man, he later would become both dean of the Georgetown University Law Center in Washington, D.C., and chairman of the Federal Trade Commission in the Clinton administration. Both private clients and government regulators frequently called upon him to comment on antitrust enforcement trends and federal regulation of the economy.

Pitofsky brought a healthy dose of reality and hands-on experience to his teaching stint at the law school, combining the rigors of legal analysis with the practical outlook of not only antitrust officials at the Department of Justice and the Federal Trade Commission but also members of Congress. He merged the theoretical and practical into one.

He was also the perfect mentor: demanding in his intellectual rigor but fair and understanding when it came to teaching a young student about the law and its complexities. Shortcuts in legal research and the preparation of antitrust memoranda were not allowed; excuses about failing to discover a recent court decision were dismissed with a warning about sloppiness and lack of attention to detail. At the same time, he welcomed the fresh outlook and creative legal analysis offered by a young law student eager to please and determined to gain his favorite professor's approval. As Pitofsky's one and only research assistant, I was invited to his home, where I met his wife, Sally, a wise southerner from Savannah, Georgia. Developing a successful working relationship with Professor Pitofsky became my top priority in law school.

An effective mentor helps a student develop a broader perspective about law and life, and reinforces certain long-held priorities, but also offers intriguing new professional and personal alternatives. A mentor helps the student develop an action plan about life. Pitofsky did all of this and more. Through him I discovered how the law really works, especially how lawmakers draft statutes and then delegate statutory interpretation, construction, and enforcement to regulators staffing executive branch agencies. Pitofsky taught me that vigorous, unbridled enforcement of the antitrust laws could be self-defeating; that political considerations, including the attitude of Congress toward such proposed enforcement, could have adverse political consequences that defeat long-term antitrust objectives. At the same time, he urged imaginative and cutting-edge thinking; if recent court decisions foreclosed one enforcement avenue, I was to consider a new road.

In my third and last year of law school, I asked Professor Pitofsky what professional options I should pursue upon graduation. My class ranking and success provided me a number of options, including working in a private law firm on Wall Street or perhaps traveling to Washington to become a young associate in the Department of Justice or at a federal regulatory agency, such as the Federal Trade Commission or the Securities and Exchange Commission. But the wise professor suggested a third option: serving for a year or two as a law clerk for a distinguished judge.

Obtaining the right coveted clerkship not only would afford me a real learning experience but also would supplement my résumé for future employment.

I suggested a few federal judges in Manhattan who might satisfy his high standards, but the savvy professor had a better idea: Why not apply for a clerkship with Stanley H. Fuld, chief judge of the New York State Court of Appeals, the highest ranking judicial officer in the state? Fuld was a nationally recognized judge and scholar, an appointee of former governor Thomas Dewey, who had written highly respected judicial opinions in such areas as criminal law, constitutional law, and choice of law. A Columbia Law School graduate (as was Pitofsky), Fuld rarely hired clerks from other than his alma mater and had never accepted a clerk from New York University. But Pitofsky urged me to make the effort and promised to write a letter of recommendation on my behalf.

What he ended up sending to Fuld was a letter to end all letters. For a page and a half, he offered Fuld various reasons why I would be a perfect fit as Fuld's clerk. Acknowledging the obvious—that Fuld's primary allegiance was to Columbia Law School—Pitofsky explained why his research assistant might prove to be an exception to the rule. As a direct result of the letter, Fuld invited me to his chambers in New York City for a personal interview. A few weeks later he called to offer me a position, explaining, "I've never hired a law clerk from New York University and I may live to regret it. But this Pitofsky letter convinces me to give it a try." I would spend the next two years as Fuld's clerk, traveling between New York City and the state capitol in Albany. The professor had come through big-time.

Before I began the clerkship, Pitofsky had one more bit of advice: he suggested that after the two-year clerkship with Fuld, I consider a career in teaching. He explained that my energy and law school success augured well if I decided to teach. He offered to help me land a position if at any time in the future I decided to follow his suggestion. Eight years later—when Professor Pitofsky had become Dean Pitofsky at Georgetown University Law Center—he again suggested it, and I became a part-time adjunct professor of law teaching mass torts and evidence or criminal law in alternate semesters.

For the next thirty years, teaching would be a vitally important part of my professional career. I welcome the opportunity to occupy center stage, to play a critical role in helping young law students learn to think like lawyers. In the classroom I control the agenda, urging students to focus not only on the intricacies and complexities of the law but also on the important public policy objectives underlying statutes and court decisions. At the same time, I can escape—even for just an hour or two—the daily pressures that confront any lawyer in day-to-day practice. Teaching law stands in stark contrast to the practical realities of professional life. I cannot imagine my legal career without teaching.

Whenever I can, I still teach one semester at Georgetown and a second semester at another distinguished law school. I also continue to seek the professor's advice at a Washington "power lunch" we enjoy together every few months. Before making any professional or personal change in course, consultation with Bob Pitofsky is a prerequisite.

The two-year judicial clerkship was every bit as valuable as Bob had predicted. I joined a small group of legal elites: present and former law clerks of Chief Judge Stanley Fuld. And shining the brightest among all of the Fuld alumni was Federal District Judge Jack B. Weinstein.

Weinstein had clerked for Fuld immediately after serving in the Navy in World War II and graduating from Columbia Law School. He had been a legal star at Columbia and was the obvious choice to clerk for Fuld. When the Fuld clerks met each year for their annual alumni dinner honoring the chief judge, Weinstein sat at the head of the table, the first among equals. Only Weinstein dared to chat casually with "Stanley"; he admired the chief judge and often commented on Fuld's legal skill. Our collective admiration for Fuld was rivaled only by our similar opinion of Weinstein.

And for good reason. A law professor at Columbia after clerking for Fuld, Weinstein has written hundreds of law review articles, speeches, essays, and commentaries on virtually every aspect of modern domestic and international law. Weinstein is still a nationally recognized legal scholar and author of definitive textbooks and legal treatises on evidence and civil procedure. His work is often cited by US Supreme Court justices in reinforcing the credibility and persuasiveness of their legal arguments. One Harvard Law School professor commented that Judge Weinstein was "the most important federal judge in the last quarter century."

But Weinstein is more than a legal scholar. Unlike Fuld, who was comfortable only in the intellectual world of the law, never straying far from his cloistered judicial chambers, Weinstein cherished the intersection of law and politics. While a law school professor, Weinstein also became active in Democratic politics, serving as county attorney for Nassau County on Long Island and later being designated an adviser to the New York Constitutional Convention in 1967. He also caught the eye of Senator Robert F. Kennedy, who recognized Weinstein's intellectual and political gifts. Kennedy suggested that President Lyndon Johnson nominate Weinstein to the federal bench, and Weinstein became a federal district judge in Brooklyn in 1967 while continuing to teach at Columbia.

Weinstein used his bully pulpit as a federal district judge to write a cascade of legal opinions on every conceivable subject. Whatever the definition of "judicial activism," he is the best, most convincing example. Undeterred by appellate court reversals of some of his more creative judicial opinions, Weinstein, who remains a sitting federal judge at the age of ninety-one, offers almost daily legal commentary that, in its force and careful legal analysis, is more convincing than anything written by the court of appeals.

My evolving professional and personal relationship with Judge Weinstein proved to be the single most important result of my Fuld clerkship. No one has had a greater direct impact on my career than Jack Weinstein. After clerking for Fuld and spending three years as an assistant US attorney in New York City, I traveled to Washington to become special counsel to Senator Ted Kennedy's Judiciary Committee. There I frequently called on Judge Weinstein for advice and guidance concerning issues pending before the committee. He was always ready to comment on committee recommendations pertaining to criminal law, regulatory reform, criminal-sentencing and bail practices, federal aid to state and local criminal justice systems, even immigration reform.

And Ted Kennedy relied on Weinstein's advice. A few years after joining Kennedy's staff, I attended a private dinner at Kennedy's home in Virginia to discuss the senator's legislative agenda. Various luminaries were invited and expected to offer their opinions. Weinstein attended and quickly became the center of attention. At one point the judge was invited to discuss the pros and cons of how judges sentence convicted offenders. At the conclusion of the dinner, Kennedy commented, "Jack, that is how all judges should think. Now I realize why my brother Bobby urged Johnson to nominate you." Weinstein became a valuable adviser to Senator Kennedy, advancing effective arguments on an almost unlimited range of federal and state law policy initiatives. On one issue after another Kennedy would say to me, "Find out what Jack thinks." Then, thanks to Judge Weinstein, came a great career-defining change. In the spring of 1984, while I was biding my time practicing law in Washington, restless for my next breakout opportunity, Weinstein invited me to his chambers in Brooklyn. He explained that he had been assigned the massive class action litigation brought by 250,000 veterans who alleged a series of physical injuries and illnesses because of exposure to the herbicide Agent Orange while serving more than a decade earlier in Vietnam. He wanted me to serve as a court-appointed mediator—"special master" in legal terminology—in an effort to resolve the case.

I accepted the assignment. As I'll explain in the next chapter, six weeks later the entire class action was settled for the unprecedented amount of $180 million. The settlement made front-page news, and my career as a mediator, negotiator, and special master began. No longer would I be just another Washington lawyer, retained by corporate clients to maneuver their way through the labyrinth that defined Washington politics. Instead I became a national mediator of choice, retained to resolve disputes that appeared hopeless and headed for years of uncertain litigation. My new professional niche was ensured.

And yet Weinstein was not finished with me. In the years to come, he called on me again and again to act as his court-appointed special master to settle other high-profile disputes in his courtroom. In 1989 it was the huge class action litigation following the closing of the Shoreham Nuclear Power Plant on Long Island. Later he appointed me to mediate settlements in thousands of asbestos death and physical injury claims, and then to help settle thousands of DES birth defect claims and other lawsuits brought by women who ingested the DES pregnancy drug and now suffered from miscarriages, cervical cancer, and other diseases. Over the next twenty-five years, the casual friendship that began with our both clerking for Judge Fuld became a lasting bond between a legal giant and his dutiful agent.

In all important matters—both professional and personal—I would not dream of making a key decision without first checking with Judge Weinstein. It is not only his legal and political skills but, more important, it is his judgment, his worldview on all issues big and small that lead me to his doorstep. Should I open a law office in New York City as well as Washington? Should I accept an invitation to teach law at a particular law school? How should I respond to an offer to return to government service at the Department of the Treasury or the Department of Justice? What questions should I ask before accepting some new public assignment? How should I handle the thorny legal and ethical issues that arise in each of the complex compensation cases recounted in this book? In these and countless other personal and professional matters, I've looked first to Judge Weinstein for advice, guidance, and friendship. And although I eventually approached Professor Pitofsky as "Bob," it frankly is still impossible for me to refer to Weinstein in any way other than "Judge." (Does anybody other than his wife, Evelyn, dare approach this imposing figure as "Jack"?)

A third valued friend has had a permanent and critically important influence on my professional career. Stephen Breyer began working for Senator Ted Kennedy in Washington in 1974, one year before I joined Kennedy's staff.

Brilliant and self-effacing, Breyer had built an impressive academic record attending Stanford University, then Harvard Law School, as well as spending time abroad studying at Oxford University. Breyer instinctively understood the interplay of law, politics, and public policy. He also was uncomfortable with the cloistered confines of academia and ambitious to be a player in fashioning public policy that could have a direct and immediate effect on people's daily lives. As a young professor at Harvard Law School, Breyer had jumped at the chance to work for a proactive senator such as Ted Kennedy. He became a consultant to Kennedy's Judiciary Committee and immediately began work on deregulating America's comfortable, inefficient, and costly airline industry. Each week Breyer would finish teaching his classes at Harvard, shuttle to Washington with his suitcase, and spend a few days in a small, cramped, indistinct Senate Judiciary Committee office. There he slowly but skillfully built the case for eliminating the Civil Aeronautics Board, while allowing the airline industry to set ticket prices tied to competition in the free market rather than the preordained rates the regulators fashioned. This emphasis on spirited competition appealed to Senator Kennedy, who saw in this subject a perfect opportunity to demonstrate his willingness to embrace the free market and laissez-faire economics, escaping the label of "big-government Democrat." (At that time Kennedy was still preserving his option of eventually running for president.)

Kennedy trusted Breyer's judgment as he trusted very few of his Senate staffers. It was not just Breyer's brilliance and credible mastery of the subject matter. He also could explain the importance of deregulation in a simple and clear manner, demonstrating how the arcane world of airline deregulation could directly and immediately affect the lives of the American people. In addition, Kennedy loved Breyer's personality, this brilliant Harvard professor who was collegial, humorous, and willing to give credit to others working on the project. Breyer proved to be the consummate team player, more than willing to defer to others, accept his role, and avoid the usual infighting found among ambitious young committee staffers. Kennedy genuinely enjoyed watching Breyer explain the technicalities of airline deregulation to other senators and their staffs. Never one to accept at face value the impractical views of academia, Kennedy viewed Breyer as an exception, a law professor with an ability to translate legal esoterica into real-world public policy. Over time he came to rely more and more on Breyer's judgment.

And when Kennedy became chairman of the Senate Judiciary Committee in 1978, Breyer was the obvious choice to be chief counsel of the committee. Breyer took a leave of absence from Harvard Law School, moved to Washington, and assumed his new role. He would not return to Harvard.

When I joined Senator Kennedy's staff after my three years as a federal prosecutor in New York City, I occupied a desk next to Breyer. I was struck by his friendliness, his savvy concerning the staff and its relationship to Kennedy, and his wise counsel on how to adjust to the time-honored procedures and protocols of the committee under its chairman, the southern baron from Mississippi, James Eastland. Breyer taught me the first rule: "No surprises! Whatever we are doing on behalf of Senator Kennedy, make sure that we consult with other committee staffers working for Eastland and the ranking Republican on the committee, Strom Thurmond. Never embarrass other members of the committee, or their staffs, with new legislative amendments or requests that have not been previously discussed. The goal is to foster transparency and a free exchange of ideas. Our word is our best weapon."

In the five years I worked for Senator Kennedy, I never forgot Breyer's wise words. When Kennedy became chairman of the committee and Breyer the chief counsel, Stephen and I would meet for breakfast every morning with Emory Sneeden, the chief minority counsel for Senator Thurmond, and plan the committee's agenda for the day. No surprises, no embarrassments. We did not always agree when it came to policy priorities for the committee or the schedule for committee hearings. But there were no hidden agendas. Open disagreements were openly resolved. This willingness on the part of Breyer and our boss, Senator Kennedy, to provide full disclosure and sunlight to the legislative process was eagerly accepted and respected by Republicans and Democrats alike on the committee. Everybody had enormous respect for Stephen Breyer: his friendliness and substantive mastery of legislation the committee was considering, his willingness to accommodate the logistical needs of other senators and their staffs (whether they required additional hires or more office space), and his flexibility in satisfying requests from other senators only increased this respect and made him the most effective chief counsel of the Senate Judiciary Committee that anybody could remember. Kennedy trusted Breyer, urging other senators, "Talk to Stephen; he'll get it done."

Observing Breyer in practice, I honed my own legislative skills. I learned that staff trust was incredibly important; deal straight with other committee staffers who are trying to satisfy their own Senate principals. Share the credit; when you do so, other staffers buy into the legislative proposal and make it their own. Develop personal relationships with other staff; accept birthday invitations, attend anniversary celebrations, and visit hospitals when a staffer is ill. Keep your work simple and easy to understand; explaining a proposed legislative amendment in a few words is preferable to a lengthy, three-page technical memorandum. Foster relationships with other senators; make sure they know who you are, who you work for, your area of expertise. (Breyer's trusted relationship with Senator Thurmond developed in part as a result of the Breyer and Thurmond families' ice skating together on weekends.) Avoid shortcuts; there is no substitute for due diligence and knowledge of the subject matter. Stay focused; work on one project at a time (as Breyer did on airline deregulation or federal criminal code reform) and avoid spreading yourself so thin that you become master of no subject, a general staffer without specialized expertise. Above all, never, ever do anything that would embarrass or surprise Senator Kennedy; your sole objective is to implement his legislative and political agenda.

My friendship with Breyer blossomed during my five years with the senator. In addition to occasional family gatherings, we consulted with each other on various wide-ranging personal issues pertaining to our careers, Senator Kennedy, and what the future might hold. We worked together on a daily basis and chatted by telephone on weekends. No major decisions were made without first exchanging views. I trust Breyer's judgment, as I have for the past thirty-five years. He has a knack for offering advice and guidance without imposing his will or insisting that his opinion is correct. His views are advisory, to be weighed in the balance; he readily admits that he might be wrong. He is there to help, not to demand. It is this approach to problem-solving and crisis management that made him such a trusted aide to Senator Kennedy and a friend I still search out for weekly or even daily advice.

His career also provides a lesson in the uncertainties of life, of roads not taken and decisions unplanned and rendered on the spur of the moment.

In the waning days of the Carter administration, a judicial vacancy was waiting to be filled on the federal First Circuit Court of Appeals in Boston. As a result of Ronald Reagan's election as the next president, it would take extraordinary political effort to fill this vacancy. Republicans in the Senate would most certainly delay any nomination President Jimmy Carter proposed. Senator Kennedy thought Professor Archibald Cox of Watergate fame just might be acceptable as a bipartisan choice. But much to his amazement and chagrin, President Carter vetoed the idea on advice from Attorney General Griffin Bell, who expressed opposition on the grounds that Cox's age (he was sixty-eight) would violate American Bar Association guidelines at the time and would establish an unfortunate precedent. I approached Breyer and suggested that with Cox out of the running, Kennedy could advance the name of the chief counsel of the Senate Judiciary Committee to fill the vacancy as a fallback. Otherwise President Reagan would have free rein to fill the vacancy with his own choice. Everybody on the Judiciary

Committee respected Breyer, and the plan just might work. Breyer gave me permission.

Senator Kennedy loved the idea. He suggested it to President Carter, who proceeded to officially nominate Breyer. After some intense politicking by Kennedy, Senator Thurmond and the other Republicans on the Judiciary Committee acquiesced in rewarding Breyer for his service, and President-elect Reagan agreed not to oppose this particular judicial nomination. The Senate quickly confirmed Breyer, who began an illustrious judicial career, first on the federal appellate court and later as a Supreme Court justice, where he remains today. It is doubtful that any of this would have happened but for President Carter's decision to reject Cox as Senator Kennedy's first choice.

Each of my mentors, Pitofsky, Weinstein, and Breyer, readily acknowledge the political genius and legislative skill of my boss, Senator Kennedy. And once you became associated with Senator Kennedy and demonstrated your worth, you were a lifelong member of the Kennedy network, ready to be called upon to offer judgment and advice at a moment's notice. If Kennedy valued your service, he would demonstrate his loyalty with public support of your career choices and with private acts of kindness. When my father became ill while vacationing in Florida, the senator arranged to have him moved to a Miami hospital for better care; when my mother visited her family in Washington, he invited her to lunch in the Senate dining room—just the two of them! She was so excited she could not finish her first course, the Senate bean soup.

If Speaker Tip O'Neill taught us that "all politics is local," it was Kennedy who confirmed that "all politics is personal." Kennedy forgot neither favors nor slights. To him, politics was a twenty-four-hour, seven-days-a-week profession. The pursuit of legislative success required that he give personal attention to his fellow senators' needs and egos. If a senator's spouse was ill, Kennedy would send a personal note and help get the spouse admitted to a preeminent hospital; all birthdays and anniversaries were acknowledged; private tours of Kennedy's museum-like Senate office were encouraged; and Kennedy would attend funerals, often delivering eulogies while offering personal condolences and assistance. An invitation to attend a private working dinner at Kennedy's home to discuss Senate priorities and legislative strategy was a very special occasion. Senate Republicans—John McCain, Ted Stevens, Lindsey Graham, Chuck Hagel, Orrin Hatch, and many others—became close personal friends. Senate Democrats, old colleagues such as Daniel Inouye and Chris Dodd, Senate leaders Tom Daschle and then Harry Reid, and newly elected senators (such as the junior senator from Illinois, Barack Obama) all sought Kennedy's advice and guidance. The evening would begin with policy discussions but would end with Kennedy inviting his Senate colleagues to join him in a song fest—invariably Irish ballads and Broadway show tunes—with Kennedy, of course, acting as choirmaster. He usually sang off key and forgot the lyrics, but nobody cared. His booming voice drowned out all others.

But Kennedy's role as a master legislative craftsman should not mask the compassion and empathy he exhibited every day in helping others, particularly his Massachusetts constituents. A few days after I undertook my responsibility for the September 11th Victim Compensation Fund, I received a request from Kennedy: Would I provide a comprehensive list of the Massachusetts residents killed when the two airplanes leaving Boston's Logan Airport crashed into the World Trade Center? He then proceeded to contact each and every Massachusetts family that had lost a loved one on 9/11, meeting personally with some and calling others. And when a Massachusetts soldier died in Desert Storm, Iraq, or Afghanistan, one might find Senator Kennedy at the funeral or grave site paying respects to the state's lost son or daughter. It was Kennedy's way.

Politics was in his blood, part of his DNA as the last Kennedy son. He remained a throwback to his brothers' time, when politics was the most noble of professions, public service both an obligation and an opportunity. Over an incredible forty-six-year Senate career, he cherished his role and labored with the burden, as keeper of the Kennedy flame, the last brother standing. He benefited from what his two brothers were denied—longevity of years—and because of this, made an impact on America and the world that arguably surpassed that of President Kennedy and Senator Robert Kennedy. (Ted Kennedy never admitted this; he spoke of President Kennedy with reverence, occasionally reminding me, "Ken, my brother was the president. I am a senator. Remember the difference.")

His legislative achievements are legendary and wide-ranging—health insurance and other social initiatives; economic help for those citizens left behind; new rights for minorities and the disabled; civil liberty protections for all; international efforts to promote peace and reduce the military arms race; reductions in nuclear weapons; support for human rights abroad. Kennedy's lasting imprint can be found in virtually every aspect of modern public life. And he accomplished all of this with a style and love of life that ensure him a prominent place in history.

During my five-year stint with Kennedy, I absorbed everything I could learn from him. His personal values became my own—empathy, compassion, the ability to compromise, preparation, determination, judgment, personal friendships and loyalty, and his warning to me: "Your word is your bond. When you give your word, honor your commitment." This last point was extremely important to Kennedy. Senator after senator would comment that when Kennedy promised to do something, he did it, regardless of political consequences. On issues such as immigration, health care, and education, once Kennedy committed to a legislative course of action—preferring compromise and give-and-take rather than the quick political sound bite—he adhered to the Senate script, standing by his Republican colleagues and Democratic allies to secure passage of important legislation. To Kennedy, "the perfect was the enemy of the good"; he always believed that in the long run of American history, and he was an integral part of that history, once you secured part of the public policy you sought, the rest would follow in time. New laws were rarely repealed; once the American people and his Senate colleagues witnessed the advantages of social legislation, expansion of the safety net would certainly follow. He believed that time was on his side. He just ran out of time.

Kennedy also taught me the advantages of sharing credit with others. Senator Chuck Hagel often told me how, in working with Kennedy on legislation, Kennedy would thrust Hagel in front of him at Senate news conferences announcing new legislative initiatives: "Chuck, get out front on this one. Take the lead; I'll stand behind you." Hagel would say with a chuckle, "Ted, you better hide; I'm not sure the citizens of Nebraska would understand the two of us standing together!" Kennedy was such a national figure, so prominent and forceful a personality, that he constantly looked for others to take the public lead in advancing a Senate cause. He disavowed Senate showmanship; he didn't need it.

My interest in public policy, in integrating my private law practice into the public arena by remaining involved in matters important to the American people, is directly attributable to Kennedy's influence and impact. He reinforced the communitarian ethic I had learned in my youth in Brockton. More than any other single individual, he urged me to make an ongoing contribution to the public good. He trained me in the psychology of public service. Whenever I accepted a new assignment and was bombarded with criticism in trying to fashion a workable solution, Kennedy's voice would echo softly in my ear: "Stay the course; do the right thing; ignore the armchair quarterbacks; get the job done; I'm standing behind you." And whenever I achieved some milestone or some professional success, Kennedy would beam with pride. I was, after all, "Kennedy-trained."

I learned at the foot of the master.

–2–

AGENT ORANGE

Compensation to Promote
Victim Solidarity

In 1979 a group of Vietnam veterans and their families filed lawsuits in courts throughout the country, claiming that the veterans had been seriously injured as a result of wartime exposure to the herbicide Agent Orange. According to the veterans, the herbicide—used as a defoliant to destroy underbrush where the enemy could hide—contained toxic dioxin, causing various ailments and injuries, some fatal. The veterans blamed the chemical companies that negligently manufactured the herbicide, as well as the Department of Defense, which sprayed the chemical despite knowing the danger. As a result, the veterans alleged a series of Agent Orange–related illnesses—cancer, scleroderma, respiratory disease, and most prominently, chloracne, a serious skin condition—and sought hundreds of millions of dollars in damages. But both the chemical industry and the US government denied liability, claiming there was no credible scientific or medical evidence that such physical injuries could be traced to Agent Orange exposure. The lawsuits constituted the largest mass tort litigation in American history; between 2 million and 3 million Vietnam veterans and from 8 million to 10 million family members might have been implicated in the litigation.

In 1984, after five years of fitful progress, the lawsuits were consolidated and sent to Judge Jack Weinstein in federal court in Brooklyn for either settlement or trial. It was not by accident that he received this assignment. Weinstein was nationally respected as a judge who knew how to manage a judicial docket. The lawyers on both sides knew Weinstein would not permit unnecessary delay or legal posturing; he would use creative judicial techniques and rulings to bring the protracted litigation to an efficient, timely conclusion. These veterans were suffering, uncertain as to when, if ever, they would receive badly needed financial help. Meanwhile, the public was watching, waiting to see whether this sad chapter in America's Vietnam experience would be brought to a fair and acceptable close.

Weinstein, himself a World War II Navy veteran, was sympathetic to the veterans' plight, but he was also troubled by the absence of credible scientific data demonstrating a link between Agent Orange exposure and the alleged injuries. He wanted to help the veterans; the question was how.

The fact is that the American tort system is ill-equipped to deal with a massive, complex medical, social, and political problem like the Agent Orange case. The time-honored adversarial system—which works well in resolving one-on-one, garden-variety disputes—practically invites delays, complications, and inefficiencies in huge complex cases as each side jockeys for advantage over the other. The burden of proof, which is (quite appropriately) placed on the plaintiffs, is so high that in a case like Agent Orange, despite the undoubted injuries and suffering of millions, it's extremely difficult to obtain redress and relief. Had Weinstein merely allowed the tort system to follow its natural course, it's likely that a massive injustice would have been done.

Rather than let that happen, he was determined to find an alternative.

In March 1984, just six weeks before the massive trial was scheduled to begin, I received a call from Weinstein, asking me to mediate a comprehensive settlement of the litigation as his court-appointed special master. I explained that I had no background whatsoever in mediation, had never been a mediator, and had never even taken a course in mediation in law school. Weinstein did not waste words: "I need somebody I can trust, somebody with the personality and skill to secure a global settlement of the litigation. Ken, you know how Washington works and have Ted Kennedy's confidence. The veterans need help and the government, especially the Veterans Administration, should be enlisted to work something out. The trial will not benefit anybody. We need to get the case settled and you are the one to do it."

Weinstein knew that such a trial could only further divide a country still reeling from the trauma of a protracted and unpopular war—it would be expensive, time-consuming, and unlikely to serve the needs of the suffering veterans. Both sides would have to settle, one way or another. It was, of course, unusual for a sitting trial judge to become as active as Weinstein in trying to promote a comprehensive settlement. Trial judges perform an important institutional role in presiding over courtroom proceedings in which lawyers engage in the give-and-take of argument, trying to convince juries of the wisdom of their conflicting views of the facts. Judges rarely become directly involved in fashioning settlements. But Agent Orange was unique, with widespread ramifications not only for the Vietnam veteran community but also for the nation. Weinstein would not sit idly by.

Adding to the complexity of the case was the awkward politics of veterans in the wake of the war. The resolution of the lawsuit could prove as sensitive a political matter as it was legally complex. Weinstein hoped that part of the settlement might include cooperation from the Veterans Administration in Washington. Medical relief and agency recognition of Agent Orange–related injuries and diseases would go a long way in easing the veterans' medical and financial uncertainty. VA action could also help provide some political legitimacy to the plight of Vietnam veterans, assisting them in their return to civilian life. So, to provide a degree of political bipartisanship to the mediation, Weinstein appointed two other Washington lawyers: David Shapiro was a prominent class action expert who knew the arcane rules governing mass tort law and the aggregation of claims; Leonard Garment, Shapiro's law partner, was a well-respected Republican who had served in the Nixon administration. Garment would provide the important ingredient of bipartisanship.

Shapiro and I did the mediating, while Garment remained in Washington and played no role thereafter. Nevertheless, the lawyers for both sides understood that it was Judge Weinstein who was pulling the strings and defining the strategy. For six weeks, as the Brooklyn trial date approached and Weinstein prepared to interview potential jurors for a trial that could take months to complete, the mediators worked around the clock, seven days a week, meeting with the lawyers separately and then together.

Lawyers for the Vietnam veterans argued that they represented sympathetic clients who had served their nation in a very unpopular war. They maintained that their scientific and medical evidence connecting Agent Orange to the alleged injuries was sufficient to at least get the case to a sympathetic jury. The defendants disagreed. The chemical industry, led by Dow and Monsanto, asserted that there was little credible scientific evidence justifying such a link. They maintained that the case would never get to a jury, that Weinstein would summarily dismiss the claims. Meanwhile, the US government hid behind absolute sovereign immunity, claiming it could not be sued in exercising its discretion to use Agent Orange to help the veterans avoid enemy ambush. The Defense Department categorically rejected becoming a defendant in the courtroom. Its legal argument was unassailable and would broker no compromise. It would not participate in any settlement of the Agent Orange litigation.

Backed by Weinstein, we mediators played each side against the other.

For hours each day, Shapiro and I met privately with the lawyers representing the veterans. A dark, empty Brooklyn courtroom with no windows was our venue of choice. We warned them that their case was woefully weak and depended on the court's willingness to let the jury hear medical testimony about the link between Agent Orange and the alleged injuries; were the lawyers willing to take the risk that Weinstein would summarily dismiss their claims? Shapiro and I took turns playing "good cop, bad cop." First Shapiro would argue that the case was weak, that even a sympathetic judge such as Weinstein would not let the jury hear it. Then I would interrupt; even if the case was heard by the jury, the appellate court likely would reject any verdict, Weinstein notwithstanding. At best, the Vietnam veterans' victory would be Pyrrhic.

We made the opposite arguments to the eight defendant chemical companies. We warned them that the court was sympathetic to the plight of Vietnam veterans and would be disinclined to deny them their day in court before a Brooklyn jury. Besides, we reminded the companies, they benefited from plenty of insurance to pay for a comprehensive settlement. Why not settle now and avoid protracted litigation with an uncertain outcome? We argued that practical business realities pointed toward a settlement.

We hammered away, day after day, week after week, trying to get the veterans and the chemical companies to agree to a comprehensive deal and avoid a trial.

In the early morning hours of May 7, 1984, just as potential jurors were ordered to court to be interviewed for the trial, and after a final all-night mediation effort, Judge Weinstein announced a comprehensive settlement. The court, the mediators, and the lawyers had not left the courthouse until after midnight the previous evening, exhausted but satisfied that a complex, uncertain trial had been avoided. Weinstein did not even bother returning to his home on Long Island, staying at a local hotel near the courthouse so he could meet with the parties and the media in open court a few hours later. Shapiro and I were buoyant; Weinstein was more measured, pleased but philosophical: "We still have a great deal of work to do convincing the veterans of the merits of the deal. Also, don't forget, the appellate courts will be reviewing our work." As we walked to the hotel the judge was already talking about the outline of his next judicial opinion approving the fairness and reasonableness of the settlement reached just minutes earlier: "We have to find a way to unite the veteran community behind this settlement."

With the mediators' help, the eight chemical company defendants agreed to pay the then-staggering sum of $180 million, plus interest, over a ten-year period to resolve all the Vietnam veteran's Agent Orange litigation. The US government was dismissed from the case and paid nothing (although the court continued to push the mediators and the government to enlist the support of the Veterans Administration in Washington). Working together, we avoided a complex and time-consuming trial in favor of a comprehensive settlement that we hoped would get money quickly to eligible Vietnam veterans and their families. As the court would later state:

> There are many considerations that make this settlement desirable from the plaintiffs' viewpoint. First, the scientific data available to date make it highly unlikely that, except perhaps for those who have or have had chloracne, any plaintiff could legally prove any causal relationship between Agent Orange and any other injury, including birth defects. Second, the law that would need to be established is unique and would almost certainly result in repeated trials and appeals, with the likely ultimate result being no recovery by any plaintiff.

Weinstein's master plan—using mediators as his agents to forge a settlement that would help Vietnam veterans, who had been criticized and maligned for serving their country—had worked. Front-page news stories and editorials championed the settlement as a practical, realistic alternative to years of litigation. And the total amount of the settlement, although small in terms of the vast dollars needed to bring needed financial relief to millions of Vietnam veterans, was unprecedented. Its sheer size helped legitimize the general plight of the veteran community in the eyes of the American people. And it helped empower the veterans—Weinstein's objective all along.

The defendant chemical companies also breathed a sigh of relief. Not only had they avoided the legal question marks inherent in an unprecedented class action litigation, but they also had succeeded in making a wise business decision. The settlement would be paid by their insurance companies with little or no bottom-line impact. And they would avoid the possibility of protracted, uncertain litigation acting as a catalyst to depress shareholder value and chill investment.

The court and the mediators had brought an end to the courtroom drama and its legal uncertainty.

But the settlement did not provide any specific guidance on distributing the proceeds among the plaintiffs. The agreement merely set forth general requirements specifying that the court would maintain and administer the settlement fund. Absent was any specific reference as to who would get what, how the money would be distributed, and which Vietnam veterans would be eligible to receive compensation.

In a creative move, Weinstein decided to hold public hearings in different locations around the country. He sincerely wanted to hear from the veterans exposed to Agent Orange. How did they propose that the settlement proceeds be distributed? The court was rightly concerned that the available settlement funds could not possibly provide meaningful compensation for all Vietnam veterans. Nor could any individual veteran demonstrate a legally acceptable link between professed injuries and illness and exposure to Agent Orange. In effect, Weinstein wanted to hear from the veterans: Who exactly should be compensated and on what basis? The settlement's legitimacy, legality, and effectiveness all depended upon answers to these questions. The court needed to develop an official record, relying upon formal testimony from the veterans themselves in deciding how to distribute settlement funds.

I took to the road with Weinstein, monitoring court hearings in New York, Chicago, Houston, Atlanta, and San Francisco. The court invited Vietnam veterans in the community to testify under oath about the settlement. And it quickly became clear how most veterans wanted the money distributed. They repeatedly focused on the plight of their "brothers," those fellow veterans most in need of financial help. At the same time, veteran after veteran—some five hundred witnesses testifying under oath—emotionally commented about their fear of birth defects affecting the unborn children of veterans exposed to Agent Orange. These veterans felt that more medical research was needed to pinpoint cause and effect. This overriding concern for others rather than themselves became the subject of often heartrending testimony from the veterans.

One veteran testified, "If all of us talking like this helps one child or one doctor to be able to pinpoint these problems and benefit one life, then I'm all for helping." Another said, "I am blessed with a healthy son and for that I thank my Higher Power. For those of my military friends who do [have children with birth defects], I know we should do what is necessary now to start the healing process." Yet another stated, "I ask this court to consider not only my family but every family so affected and set aside at least one half of the total final settlement for the children and their children's children."

Such a fund was a popular idea across the board. One speaker admitted, "The newly acquired monies from the lawsuit would mean nothing to me, but continued research into dioxin-related illnesses could help thousands of others, and a fund started to aid that research would be a fitting tribute to the many who suffered for their participation in the Vietnam War." According to another, "The answer is to provide a means whereby adequate medical care is made available to Vietnam veterans. . . . The monies in this settlement could be used as a part of a fund set up for this reason." And one vet summed up the thinking of thousands when he said, "Let us be done with the delays and begin now to create programs and provide services to assist present and future generations affected."

This testimony from the Vietnam veterans was directly at odds with their lawyers' opinions. Trained in the tradition of the common law of torts, the lawyers submitted to the court a proposed distribution plan at the conclusion of the hearings, urging Weinstein to approve a hierarchy of eligible illnesses tied to Agent Orange exposure. Based upon the available medical and scientific evidence the lawyers cited, Vietnam veterans with certain diseases would receive a preference over other veterans with more problematic claims for compensation.

Weinstein would have none of it. He reminded the lawyers that the science and medicine connecting Agent Orange to disease were uncertain, incomplete, and contradictory. More important, Weinstein was troubled by the implications of the lawyers' argument. A hierarchy of diseases linked to Agent Orange would fuel divisiveness and provoke argument among the very veterans he was trying to help. Weinstein understood human nature; a settlement distribution plan should not pit one veteran against another—and if it were designed according to the strictures of tort law, it would do exactly that. Any settlement had to help heal the wounds associated with the Vietnam War, not exacerbate them.

Weinstein sat with me in his chambers in Brooklyn: "We need to develop a creative, workable settlement program that will help the veterans and avoid finger-pointing. The testimony of the veterans points the way. You should develop and submit a distribution plan that has the veterans' support even if it is unconventional. Don't rely just on tort law. Go a different route."

This was bold, innovative thinking by a very determined court. I reminded the judge that I knew of no precedent for establishing settlement criteria in a tort case that did not rely on tort principles of causation and damage. He said with a chuckle, "Think like Stanley Fuld, Ken; let's use the law to find a better way. Tort law will divide the Vietnam veterans. Besides, no veteran can prove causation; that is why they settled the case."

For the next few weeks I mulled over various options and possibilities, trying to fashion a plan that would satisfy the veterans but would also pass muster in any court of appeals that would review the plan. Constantly exchanging ideas with Weinstein, I sought an answer to a vexing question: If no individual Vietnam veteran could legally satisfy the court that Agent Orange had caused his illness, what objective criteria would substitute for conventional cause and effect?

Finally I submitted an official plan of distribution that addressed the court's concerns but still would find political support from the veterans. The compensation program would be divided into two parts: the bulk of the settlement proceeds would go to veterans exposed to Agent Orange while serving in Southeast Asia who subsequently died or now suffered the most disabling physical injuries; the remainder of the funds would be used to establish a foundation (Agent Orange Class Assistance Program), which would fund programs and projects generally designed to assist Vietnam veterans and their families. The proposed plan would provide individual checks to the most disabled veterans, while also assisting the remaining members of the class through the creation and funding of social service, medical assistance, and veteran advocacy programs.

Lawyers representing the veterans were not pleased. This solution flew in the face of all they had learned in law school about the legal necessity of proving cause and effect when it came to injury and death. Why should a disabled Vietnam veteran be able to receive compensation without first showing that his physical plight was caused by exposure to Agent Orange? The lawyers were appalled at this effort to do an end run around two hundred years of tort law. At the same time, they opposed creating a fund providing general social service assistance to other Vietnam veterans, a well-intentioned but unprecedented idea with no basis in the law. The lawyers vowed to fight my creative proposal.

But Judge Weinstein remained on my side. In a ringing endorsement, the court made clear the road it would take. After rejecting suggestions the veterans' lawyers offered, Weinstein stated:

A number of other suggestions are discussed below. None has as much merit as that proposed by Special Master Kenneth R. Feinberg, Esq. In an elegant solution, he suggests a combination of insurance-type compensation to give as much help as possible to individuals who, in general, are most in need of assistance, together with a foundation run by veterans with the flexibility and discretion to take care of individuals and groups most in need of help. With some slight modifications, the Special Master's recommendations are adopted.

The court rejected the time-honored foundation of tort law the plaintiff lawyers advanced:

> In the case of Agent Orange implementation of any distribution plan based on traditional tort principles is impossible because of virtual absence of proof of causation, financially impracticable because of administrative costs, and not feasible for other compelling reasons. . . . The only realistic means of proceeding with the distribution that sufficiently addresses these concerns is embodied in the Special Master's Report. . . . Under this plan only totally disabled veterans and the surviving spouses or children of deceased veterans will receive individual cash awards. The class as a whole, however, will benefit significantly in other ways [from the Agent Orange Class Assistance Program].

And what were the "slight modifications" the court made to my "elegant solution"? Weinstein recognized that it was not practical or wise to determine eligibility based strictly on death or degree of disability while completely ignoring all requirements of conventional tort causation. He expressed concern, for example, that certain emotionally charged veterans suffering from mental illness might commit suicide to help their families receive compensation. He also refused to declare eligible those Vietnam veterans who, although exposed to Agent Orange and now totally disabled, were also the victims of automobile accidents, gunshot wounds, and other traumatic injuries. These veterans might claim that such accidents were tied to Agent Orange exposure, but the court drew the line at illnesses (eligible) as opposed to traumatic injuries (ineligible). Traditional principles of tort causation would play a limited role in tempering the special master's proposed plan.

The court's approach to compensating these veterans clearly answered the question: Who gets what? Weinstein's pioneering decision rejected the formalities of much of existing tort law to help the Vietnam veterans and families most in need. Totally disabled veterans or the families of deceased veterans who had been exposed to the defoliant while serving in Vietnam would be paid; others would not. Individual tort causation principles would largely be ignored. But other veterans, although ineligible to receive individual payments, at least would receive some degree of social service assistance from the foundation the class action settlement established. The foundation would ensure that, at least in theory, all Vietnam veterans would benefit from the settlement even if only a modest few would receive a check in the mail. The court was determined to address the plight of Vietnam veterans who served in an unpopular war and were finding it difficult to transition back into everyday American life. The settlement would, in a modest way, bring some financial relief to the Vietnam veteran community. More important, it would signal to Washington, especially the Veterans Administration, that these veterans' needs could not be ignored. (Sadly, only years later would the VA, acting pursuant to statute, officially recognize Agent Orange exposure as justifying the full panoply of veterans' benefits.)

Over the program's ten-year life, the $180 million settlement grew, with interest, to $243 million. About $178 million of this eventually was distributed to 52,000 individual veterans and their families, while $42 million was used to fund various legal, social, and medical programs to assist the families of Vietnam veterans. It also funded programs to educate the Vietnam veteran community concerning the availability of government benefits, conducted national conferences and meetings to reinforce veteran solidarity, and paid for lawsuits challenging the VA's Agent Orange regulations (the courts ultimately determined that the VA had in fact discriminated against Vietnam veterans in certain regulations). The remainder of the settlement proceeds went to pay lawyers and related trial expenses.

The Agent Orange settlement is, of course, the poster child of "judicial activism," perhaps the best example of judicial engineering by a brilliant jurist determined to bring some degree of relief and recognition to the often maligned and ostracized community of Vietnam veterans. If it is a personal achievement of Judge Weinstein, it is also the high-water mark of mass tort aggregation and settlement, a singular example that has not been replicated in the nearly thirty years since it was announced. Subsequent efforts to use the class action device to resolve asbestos and tobacco litigation have been unsuccessful. The courts, including the US Supreme Court, have concluded that such aggregative litigation is unwise and cannot be legally justified. The cases are too idiosyncratic, too different, too individualized, too sprawling in cause and effect to justify class action certification. Weinstein's opinion in Agent Orange stands alone as a beacon to guide adventurous, creative lawyers who seek to stretch the outer bounds of the law to accomplish justice.

The court of appeals made certain that Weinstein's Agent Orange opinion would not be a precedent. Even while approving the court's revolutionary handiwork, it warned that this settlement was limited to the facts and circumstances of the post-Vietnam era. The reason: this settlement "justifies the prevalent skepticism over the usefulness of class actions in so-called mass tort cases and, in particular, claims for injuries resulting from toxic exposure." The appellate court expressed concern that if other courts followed Weinstein's leadership, it "would inject the judicial branch into political and military decisions that are beyond its constitutional authority and institutional competence." In effect, the court would approve one and only one Agent Orange settlement; it would not be so favorably disposed if the "son of Agent Orange" was presented. Other courts duly heeded this warning

It is important, however, to recognize the settlement's bold and innovative nature. Weinstein found a way to avoid worsening the divisiveness and anger that already characterized much of the Vietnam veteran community by first traveling around the country to hear from the veterans themselves. Then, building upon that information and largely ignoring the arguments of the lawyers trained in the conventional, the court developed a plan that would promote the political solidarity and cohesiveness of the Vietnam veteran community. Far from encouraging anger and finger-pointing, it would rally the veterans around a common cause. Yes, the individual payments would be modest (a clear indication that the settlement's overall value reflected the weaknesses of the lawsuit). But in a very real sense, the money was secondary; the court (and the veterans themselves) viewed the settlement as a vindication of their suffering, and as an important step on their road to recovery. In addition, the settlement would demonstrate that governmental institutions, in this case the courts, could be responsive to Vietnam veterans seeking nothing more than to return to America as partners in good standing.

The Agent Orange settlement, therefore, must be viewed primarily as an important concluding chapter in America's sad Vietnam experience. It should be studied and analyzed in that context, and that context alone. The court stepped up when other institutions of government were frozen in place, paralyzed by the legacy of Vietnam. If the court's answer to the question of who gets what was unique, unprecedented, and unlikely to be repeated, it was, nevertheless, the perfect answer at a time when America and Vietnam veterans were struggling to cope with the war's aftermath. Judge Weinstein was in the right place at the right time. Individual compensation tied to death and disability; modest payments; and a program created to help Vietnam veterans were important antidotes to combat the sense of uncertainty and concern that characterized the Vietnam veteran community, and America itself, after the war.

Weinstein had approved an unprecedented settlement despite reservations grounded in traditional tort concepts of cause and effect. He was not about to approve a plan that would run counter to the concerns expressed during the fairness hearings he conducted throughout the nation. From the very beginning his strategy was to unite the already battered and frustrated Vietnam veteran community in a common cause, not to further divide it.

The court's opinion approving the settlement was vintage Weinstein. He would bend the law to meet the Vietnam veteran community's needs—as expressed by the veterans themselves. Refusing to be constrained by legal precedent, he stretched the boundaries of the law to achieve the "right result." These veterans had suffered enough. He would do what he could to right the balance.

And yet even as the legal implications remained firmly rooted in Vietnam, the lessons of this experience informed my work for decades to come—and two decades later, when I was called once again to determine who got what after great tragedy, Weinstein's example would prove a vital inspiration.

– 3 –

THE SEPTEMBER 11TH
VICTIM COMPENSATION FUND

———

Public Compensation for a
Special Group of Victims

Just eleven days after the September 11, 2001, terrorist attacks, Congress passed a law without precedent in American history. Technically labeled the Air Transportation Safety and Systems Stabilization Act, the new statute provided financial support and loan guarantees to the domestic airline industry, staggered by the events at the World Trade Center, the Pentagon, and Shanksville, Pennsylvania.

In the chaos and confusion following the national tragedy, the airline industry had rushed to Congress for help. Its representatives warned that in the wake of the attacks, the public would shun domestic and international airline travel. The industry pleaded for financial protection, demanding that the government limit victims' rights to sue the airlines for negligence. Congress quickly responded. But it did not upend the legal system completely; victims and their families still could file private tort lawsuits against the airlines, the World Trade Center, and other potential defendants, but only in federal court in Manhattan, not in state courts (with more sympathetic jurors) closer to the victims' home. And airline financial liability would be limited to $6 billion, the total amount of insurance available for the four planes the terrorists hijacked. By capping the airlines' potential financial liability, Congress was sending a clear signal to victims and lawyers alike: think twice before litigating; it is not in America's interest for the airline industry to become a courtroom target.

But in an eleventh-hour move, after just one day of debate, Congress inserted into the law, as an afterthought, Title IV, which established a compensation fund for the victims of the attacks and their families. If Congress was going to limit lawsuits, it was only fair to provide an alternative method for compensating eligible claimants.

This new title offered the families of those who died on 9/11, and those victims who survived with horrible physical injuries, two alternatives: They could file lawsuits in federal court in New York City claiming that the airlines, the World Trade Center, the airplane manufacturers, and others were negligent in not preventing the attacks, and hope for a home run in the courtroom. Or they could waive their right to sue and opt into a publicly funded compensation program where the claimant would not need to prove defendant liability but only show that the deaths and injuries resulted from the attacks. The choice was theirs.

According to the new statute, the compensation would be tax free and would consist entirely of public taxpayer money. Neither the airline industry, nor the World Trade Center, nor any other defendant company would be required to contribute one cent to the new fund. Nor did Congress appropriate any fixed amount to pay the victims; uncertain as to how lives should be valued for purposes of payment, it simply transferred the issue to a special master who would design and administer the program with delegated authority from the US attorney general. This special master would have largely unfettered discretion in evaluating claims and compensating victims from petty cash sitting in the US Treasury. Congress abdicated any role whatsoever in implementing the compensation program. In an emotional rush to pay eligible victims, it designated the attorney general to select the special master without the formalities of Senate confirmation.

This degree of delegation—from Congress to the attorney general to a designated special master—was unprecedented. Yet it was understandable. Congress was determined to act, and act fast. It wanted compensation paid to 9/11 victims as soon as possible. To avoid procedural niceties, which undoubtedly would delay the payments, it opted for speed. A single individual would have the authority to design and administer the new program.*

No statute in American history posed greater challenges in determining who got what than this new law. In the months following the 9/11 attacks, a single special master first would define eligibility—deciding exactly who could file a claim and who could be paid (not

---

*A thorough rendering of my tenure as special master of the September 11th Victim Compensation Fund is addressed in my earlier book, *What Is Life Worth?* There, I recite in more detail my appointment by the US attorney general and my service as special master.

always the same person). Second, the special master would calculate appropriate damages for each of the thousands of claimants. He, and he alone, then would decide appropriate compensation—two formidable tasks, and an enormous responsibility.

When I read about the new statute establishing the 9/11 fund, I was immediately intrigued. I contacted my old friend Republican Senator Chuck Hagel of Nebraska. We had worked together during my Agent Orange days when Hagel had been a deputy administrator of the Veterans Administration. In turn, Hagel telephoned the Department of Justice, and within a few days I was interviewed by Attorney General John Ashcroft. It quickly became apparent that we saw eye to eye on the task at hand. Ashcroft warned me about the difficulties that would accompany decisions compensating emotional victims and their families. There had never been a statute like this. But the attorney general was impressed with my credentials and experience. Meanwhile, it didn't hurt that I had been a key aide to Senator Ted Kennedy; the political risks associated with administering the new statute required Ashcroft to appoint a special master far removed from the Bush administration. After a second interview, he offered me the job.

I ended up spending thirty-three months as special master of the September 11th Victim Compensation Fund. I paid more than $7 billion to approximately 5,500 claimants representing the dead and physically injured. The stories I heard from the families and surviving victims haunt me even a decade later.

In fashioning compensation programs, I am always asked: How do you go about deciding who gets what? What issues do you confront in deciding both eligibility and the amount to be paid? The September 11th Victim Compensation Fund is the perfect prototype for addressing these questions. It vividly illustrates the surprising complexities inherent in answering these seemingly simple questions.

First, as for who would get compensated, Title IV set out in limited detail the eligibility criteria. The families of those killed on the airplanes or at the World Trade Center or Pentagon could file a claim; so could those who were physically injured in the "immediate vicinity" of the attacks (although what exactly this phrase meant was left vague—how "immediate"? what "vicinity"?). Those victims alleging purely mental injury, without an accompanying physical injury, were ineligible even if they escaped the horror through sheer luck or happenstance and were now incapacitated because of depression or other mental suffering.

But the statute was silent when it came to the very important question of exactly which particular family members were eligible to apply to the fund or receive compensation. In its rush to enact the new law and demonstrate its support and compassion for the victims and their families, the Congress had neglected to deal with a precise definition of "who." Instead it left answers to these issues to the attorney general and his special master to work out in subsequent regulations and case-by-case determinations.

What if the surviving spouse or parents of the victim could not agree? What if siblings were at odds? What about fiancés and same-sex partners? Fund regulations would, by necessity, have to address these issues. If the victim had executed a will, we usually would follow the will's directions; if there was no will, we would look to the state law of the victim's domicile to determine who could file and who would be eligible to receive fund proceeds. State law, therefore, would help determine the definitions surrounding eligibility.

Working with key officials at both the Department of Justice and the Office of Management and Budget, I set about drafting 9/11 fund regulations to implement the statutory directive. For six weeks a small working group met around a large conference table at the Justice Department sharing drafts of the regulations, trying to figure out how to resolve thorny issues about eligibility, the size of awards, and a host of related issues. We circulated drafts to interested officials throughout the department and the Office of Management and Budget. Once we agreed, interim regulations were officially declared in the Federal Register and disseminated to the public for comment. Eventually a final rule announced a comprehensive set of 9/11 fund regulations.

The eligibility criteria for death claims posed no difficulty; death certificates from the New York City Police Department, passenger manifests from the four ill-fated airplanes, and military records from the Pentagon helped define which families could apply for fund death benefits.

Physical injury claims were more problematic. I quickly recognized that if the regulations were not narrowly drawn, the fund might receive millions of claims from residents of New York City boroughs and New Jersey claiming respiratory injury arising from the smoke, dust, and debris emanating from the collapsed World Trade Center towers. In the days following the attacks, newspaper accounts featured stories of panicked residents of Staten Island and Jersey City complaining of repeated coughing and hacking from breathing the foul air. I was also concerned that latent physical injury claims might not be submitted until weeks, months, or even years after the attacks.

We crafted fund regulations that addressed these problems. First, since the statute limited claims to the "immediate vicinity" of the terrorist attacks, the regulations required that World Trade Center physical injury claims be limited by geography; the boundaries for eligibility would be Canal Street to the north, West Street and Lower Broadway to the west and east, and South Ferry to the south. Residents across the Hudson River or living in the other New York City boroughs were ineligible. The regulations also required that any valid claims of physical injury be accompanied by medical records that confirmed emergency treatment within seventy-two hours of the September 11 attacks (ninety-six hours for first responders, who were too busy to seek earlier medical help). If the victim asserted a latent physical injury, these time restrictions would begin to run from the date the alleged disease first became apparent. These criteria would drastically curtail the potential scope of the statute and the number of eligible physical injury claims.

After determining who would get compensation, the next challenge was deciding the amount. This issue raised a host of fresh complications. The statute declared that damages would be tort based. That meant that the special master first would calculate the economic loss the victims suffered—what the victims would have earned over a lifetime but for the terrorists—then would add to this calculation some amount for noneconomic loss (the pain and suffering and emotional distress visited on the victims and their loved ones). Finally, the new law required that the special master deduct from any final award collateral sources of income the victims and their families received, such as proceeds from life insurance and workers' compensation programs.

The economic loss determinations were relatively straightforward and were based on traditional time-honored tort concepts. How old was the victim? What was the victim earning at the time of death or injury? What did Department of Labor and Bureau of the Census statistics say about the likely retirement age of victims working in particular occupations and professions? Courts and juries in every city and village in the nation made these types of determinations every day. The special master would assume the role of both judge and jury in making such calculations for each claimant.

But by tying the calculation of compensation to the tort system and its concept of economic loss, the statute guaranteed that every eligible claimant would receive a *different* amount of money. It was a critical flaw in the program's design. The families of the banker, the stockbroker, and the lawyer who were killed while working in the financial services offices on the upper stories of the World Trade Center would receive higher awards than those of the waiter working in the Windows on the World restaurant, the military officer stationed at the Pentagon, and the firefighter or the police officer who responded to the attacks. This, of course, made sense since the statute's purpose was to entice individual victims out of the courtroom, urging them instead to seek compensation from the new fund. The special master would have to pay the stockbroker's family much more than the family of the firefighter if this family was to voluntarily surrender its right to sue.

But by paying every claimant a different amount of public taxpayer money, the new statute promoted divisiveness and anger among the very individuals Congress was trying to help. As one irate widow stated, "This law is ridiculous! My husband was a fireman and died a hero at the World Trade Center. The statute will give me $2 million. But my next-door neighbor, who was a banker working for Enron, will get $3 million! Why is the government doing this?" The new law might provide generous public compensation to each eligible claimant, but every claimant would shop and compare. Absolute dollars would be overshadowed by comparisons.

And what about noneconomic loss? The pain and suffering of the victim, and the emotional distress visited on surviving families, posed thorny problems. The tort system gives judges and juries wide discretion in making these determinations; a victim who suffers for a few extra minutes before death might receive millions of dollars more in noneconomic loss than the victim who was killed instantly. Each individual plaintiff receives tailored treatment in the courtroom depending upon the nature of the evidence and the circumstances surrounding the death.

Should the special master follow tort law to the letter and offer different amounts to each claimant depending on the amount of time the victim suffered prior to death? Should the victims killed instantly at the World Trade Center receive less compensation than the passengers on the airplanes who suffered unimaginable fear and terror as the planes headed for the World Trade Center and the Pentagon?

I ultimately decided to deal with this emotional subject by rejecting the tort system's approach. The 9/11 fund was not dealing with isolated individual death cases in the courtroom but rather with almost 3,000 traumatic deaths all occurring within a matter of minutes. For the fund to even attempt to calibrate individual claims of pain and suffering would cause emotional turmoil, with each distraught surviving family member submitting horrific evidence of a loved one's likely last few minutes on the airplanes, or at the World Trade Center or Pentagon. Why make families go through this exercise? It was settled: just as Judge Jack Weinstein had done for Agent Orange, we would leave behind the tort system's formula. Instead the regulations would apply a uniform formula treating all families the same when it came to noneconomic loss— an award of $250,000 for a 9/11 death and an additional $100,000 for each surviving spouse and dependent. No additional evidence of pain and suffering or emotional distress would be required, no horrific narrative of a victim's likely last few minutes. The fund would try to discourage emotional reflections of that tragic day from vulnerable surviving families.

There was also the problem of deducting collateral sources of income resulting from the terrorist attacks. Congress had decided that public monies should be used only as a last resort and that other sources of compensation should be deducted in making the calculations. This made sense if the objective was to ensure a financial safety net for survivors confronting future economic uncertainty. But it did not sit well with those applying to the fund, as suggested by one typical, understandable complaint:

> Mr. Feinberg, I don't get it. My wife and I planned our financial future by making sure we purchased life insurance. Our next-door neighbors didn't buy life insurance, but instead took the life insurance premium money and splurged at Las Vegas. Why are you deducting my $1 million life insurance proceeds, while my next-door neighbor benefits from having no life insurance? It makes no sense.

I tried to explain the language of the statute, but obviously this left claimants unsatisfied. So I used my broad discretion in calculating bottom-line dollars—permitted by both the statute and the regulations—to temper the harshness of the collateral source rule.

And what about the generous payments paid to victims by private charitable organizations, such as the American Red Cross, the Robin Hood Foundation, and the Twin Towers Fund? Should these contributions, totaling well over $2 billion, also be deducted from any final 9/11 fund awards? The statute certainly could be read as requiring these deductions. But to keep their funds from being used merely to offset taxpayer dollars, the charities began threatening to withhold any additional payments to eligible victims until after the 9/11 fund had issued its awards. After meeting with representatives of these charities, I decided not to treat private charitable payments as collateral sources of income. I had no intention of being held responsible for delaying these private payments to distressed families and surviving victims.

Resolving these issues—fund eligibility requirements, the damage calculations incorporating concepts of economic and noneconomic loss, defining collateral source deductions—ultimately determined who got what. The 9/11 fund remains a textbook example of how to design a public compensation program by addressing a lockstep series of issues.

But one other important consideration, due process and procedural fairness, also entered the mix. Affording every claimant the opportunity to be heard was essential to the fund's success. The option would be entirely voluntary; no claimant was required to meet with me. But if survivors wanted to exercise their option and give testimony under oath about the death of a loved one, or about the effort to survive and move forward with horrible, disfiguring physical injuries, the 9/11 fund would welcome the opportunity to meet with them.

Over the thirty-three-month life of the program I personally conducted more than 900 of these hearings. The subject was rarely compensation. Individual claimants were reluctant to even raise the issue; instead, time and again they focused on the memory of a lost loved one, on the desire to validate a life now tragically ended without advance notice or warning.

Many of the statements still ring in my memory:

There is no greater love than the unconditional love between a parent and a child. . . . When he would be out late at night, I couldn't sleep. Then I would hear him park his car and climb into the basement window with a great feeling to know he was home. It takes a parent to know that feeling. . . . I think of him when we see his friends getting married and having children together, and then I think our family has one child missing. . . . My son . . . meant the world to me. He'll always be my little boy. I miss him more than words can ever say. He was one of the greatest joys of my life, and I'll always love him.

The loss is not the greatest for me; I had five years with [my husband]. . . . I remember having so many dreams where he would come and take [our son] from me and [my husband] would say, "Just give me five minutes. I just need five minutes and I'll give him back." And if I could give him five minutes, I'd give him five minutes, because he never had anything.

I have a very strong faith, and he's always around me, so that helps me as well . . . because there are people that believe dead is dead, gone is gone. I don't believe that. I believe he's right now with me, and I believe he walks with me every step of the way, and that gives me strength. But he was such an incredibly strong person in what he did, not only on that day, but in his life, that I owe it to him to try and be as strong as I can as well.

I will never forget one hearing in particular. A young woman came to see me, distraught, sobbing and on the verge of collapse. She explained that she had lost her husband at the World Trade Center:

Mr. Feinberg, my husband was "Mr. Mom." Every day that he was not at the office, he was home, teaching our six-year-old how to play baseball, teaching our four-year-old how to read, reading a bedtime story to our two-year-old. And what a chef! He was also the gardener mowing the lawn. He was "Mr. Mom." The only reason I am still on this earth and have not joined him in heaven is because of our three children. He would want me to stay here because of the children.

She left. The next day I received a telephone call from a lawyer in New York City:

Mr. Feinberg, did you meet yesterday with a woman with three children who lost her husband at the World Trade Center? I don't want to complicate your life. You have a very difficult job. *But she doesn't know that her husband had two other children with his girlfriend in the Bronx.* I represent the girlfriend. When you issue your 9/11 fund check, there are not three surviving children, but rather five children. I will be able to prove paternity. I'm sure you will do the right thing.

Stories like this kept me awake at three A.M. Should I tell the widow about the two other children in the Bronx? Would it help her to know the facts? Even if it would be beneficial, was I the right person to explain the situation? I decided to keep quiet. I did not know all of the facts or the circumstances. I was not a family or marriage counselor. My job was to compensate the 9/11 victims. The woman had an opinion about her late husband. In her grief, I thought it inappropriate to add to her turmoil.

I authorized two separate confidential awards: one for the widow and her three children, and one for the girlfriend, guardian of the decedent's two children. Now, over ten years later, the widow probably knows about her late husband's previous life and his two other children. But I continue to believe I made the right decision.

As a result of these and other hearings, my office was swamped with memorabilia claimants sent me to corroborate their reflections about a victim murdered on 9/11: awards, medals, diplomas, ribbons, certificates of good conduct, letters, proclamations. All were submitted with one purpose in mind: to help the special master appreciate the good character and selflessness of the departed.

Because the hearing process was manageable and administratively convenient, these intimate, one-on-one hearings proved a valuable tool in empowering claimants and affording them a stake in the process. But I always knew that the hearings were a luxury made possible by the relatively limited number of claimants. As claim volume increases, and a compensation program is over-whelmed by thousands or tens of thousands of individuals seeking payment, such individual hearings become impractical, a source of delay and inefficiency, as I later realized when administering the Gulf Coast Claims Facility arising out of the BP oil spill in the Gulf of Mexico.

If one looks at statistics alone, the September 11th Victim Compensation Fund can be viewed only as a resounding success. In the end, each family that lost a loved one in the attacks received an average compensation of $2 million. Those who suffered disabling injuries received payments averaging $400,000. Some 98 percent of all eligible surviving families voluntarily opted into the fund; only ninety-four families decided to sue the airlines and the World Trade Center rather than accept a fund award. (Years later all of these families settled out of court. Although these settlements are confidential, it is fair to conclude that after deducting legal fees, litigation costs, and the time value of money, most received net amounts less than the tax-free amounts the fund provided.)

The public also embraced the fund's success. My concern that the nation's taxpayers would recoil at the special master's paying billions to 9/11 victims and their families proved entirely unjustified. Instead the public endorsed the program's generosity, expressing support for the effort to come to the aid of those who, through no fault of their own, had become victims. Now, more than a decade since the terrorist attacks, strangers still stop me in airline terminals and on city streets to thank me for taking on such a tough assignment and for being so generous. Recognizing me from television appearances and newspaper photos, citizens who comment are always gracious and supportive: "Aren't you the fellow who paid the victims of the 9/11 attacks? Thank you for your service. I don't know how you did it."

But was the September 11th Victim Compensation Fund sound public policy? How does one justify a program that provides generous tax-free public compensation to a narrowly defined number of victims while denying similar generosity to those suffering similar loss? There was no 9/11-type fund for the victims of the Oklahoma City terrorist attack, the suicide attack directed at the USS *Cole* in Yemen, or for those who died in the original 1993 attack at the World Trade Center, committed by the same type of terrorists. Why not?

Nor is the problem limited to the fallout caused by terror. Congress fell silent when it came to considering compensation for the victims of Hurricane Katrina in 2005, or the tornados that ravaged Tuscaloosa, Alabama, and Joplin, Missouri in 2011. By any definition, these were mass disasters. And what about individual innocent victims of an isolated tragedy—the woman who rescued three little girls from the Mississippi River, only to drown after saving them; the young law student minding her own business while walking on a city sidewalk, only to be killed by a hit-and-run drunken driver; the firefighter and police officer who, like those first responders at the World Trade Center, place their lives at risk every day in the service of their local communities? Why no check for each of them?

How does one justify—if indeed one can do so—a generous public compensation program limited to a select few? The September 11th Victim Compensation Fund calls into question the very idea of "who gets what?"

Over the past decade I have repeatedly stated, and continue to believe, that the 9/11 fund was sound public policy, that it was a justified compassionate response by the American people to an unprecedented national tragedy. Immediately after the attacks, as emotions (including patriotic fervor) ran high, Congress wanted to demonstrate to the world its empathy and support for the victims. Staggered by this foreign attack on American shores, Congress quickly enacted a generous, publicly funded compensation program as proof positive that Americans stood together, a single community ready to help one another in our collective hour of need. From the perspective of the American people—not the perspective of the individual victims themselves—the 9/11 fund helped the nation cope with the tragedy.

In studying the language of the new law that created the fund, I was reminded of the Lincoln Memorial in Washington, D.C. One of Abraham Lincoln's fists is clenched tight, evidence of his determination to do whatever is necessary to save the Union. But his other fist is open, reaching out to all the victims of the Civil War, a symbol of the nation's compassion and obligation to help one another, whether from North or South. So it was in the weeks following the 9/11 attacks. The nation's might would be used to track down Osama bin Laden and the terrorists who planned the attacks; at the same time, the people of the United States would come to the aid of citizens in distress. Americans realized the randomness of life and death; they themselves could have been victims on that day.

It is, of course, true that the 9/11 fund was created largely to discourage lawsuits that could bring the airlines to their knees. But Congress could have bailed out the airlines without providing such generous compensation funded entirely by the taxpayer. The 9/11 fund is best read as an emotional, spur-of-the-moment act of patriotism and empathy for our fellow citizens. If Congress had waited two more weeks before considering the wisdom of the 9/11 fund, I doubt it would have created such a generous public compensation program. But time was of the essence. And at this exact time and place in our history, Congress acted appropriately. The American people can look back more than ten years later and point with pride to such a fund.

But Congress should not do it again. The very idea of creating a tax-free public compensation program for a limited group of citizens, each receiving a different amount, while denying similar generosity to others, is inconsistent with an American political philosophy characterized by equal protection of the laws and a sense of egalitarianism and fair play. Our political character frowns on elitism, the idea that government should help a favored few while leaving others to fend for themselves. Notions of self-reliance and individual freedom—to make choices as to where we will live, how we will act, what dangers we will confront, and how we will react to adversity—are essential parts of our American heritage. Limited government means just that. We do not seek, or even anticipate, a generous financial handout from the government every time tragedy strikes. Private insurance and individual planning for life's uncertainties are the rule, grafted in the consciousness of the American people over the past two centuries.

What makes the 9/11 fund so unique is the generosity of the compensation and that it was financed entirely by the taxpayer. These two facts pose an insurmountable burden to citing the fund as a precedent.

A few years ago I was invited to England to meet with a few members of Parliament who were interested in compensating the victims of terrorist attacks directed at the London public transportation system. The meeting was cordial and all went well until one member inquired about the levels of compensation. He was shocked to hear the truth: "Your government paid how much?!" The meeting soon ended. Similarly, in 2007 I traveled to Canberra, Australia, to meet with elected officials considering public compensation for the victims of the nation's tragic past policy toward relocating aborigines. Again, the discussions reached a standstill once they learned about the amounts the 9/11 fund paid to victims.

But Congress's decision to tie 9/11 compensation to the tort system by encouraging eligible claimants to voluntarily waive their right to sue guaranteed the extraordinary generosity of the payments. The tort system and the 9/11 fund were joined at the hip. Although this was unfortunate—Congress could have exhibited its compassion and empathy by providing each victim the same flat amount regardless of occupation or personal circumstance—the very genesis of the fund arose out of congressional efforts to discourage lawsuits. Accomplishing the latter required tying the payments to the very tort system Congress sought to avoid. Because England and Australia did not embrace a similar legal system (public officials in London and Canberra were amazed at the vagaries, inefficiencies, and uncertainties of our trial courts), there was no reason to authorize such extraordinarily generous payments.

Nor should the 9/11 fund serve as a precedent here at home. Congress certainly has expressed no interest in replicating the fund to deal with other natural or man-made disasters. Occasionally officials of private pharmaceutical or manufacturing corporations ask me whether the 9/11 fund might be useful as a precedent to deal with mass tort litigation involving drugs, medical devices, asbestos, silica, and other products generating thousands of lawsuits. My answer is always the same: "Yes, the 9/11 fund can be a precedent. Just provide $2 million for each death and ask the taxpayers to pay for it!" The idea is dead on arrival. It would take an extraordinary, unprecedented amount of private corporate generosity for this type of fund to have any legs. As Chapter 6 will highlight, BP's unprecedented pledge of $20 billion to pay for financial and ecological damage caused by the oil rig explosion in the Gulf of Mexico in April 2010 stands alone in this regard.

However, recent legislation has given the 9/11 fund new life. In January 2011, during the last congressional lame-duck session, a new statute was passed reopening the September 11th Victim Compensation Fund to deal with thousands of police officers, firefighters, construction workers, and other first responders who toiled at the World Trade Center in the weeks and months following the attacks. Like those thousands of responders who suffered physical injury immediately after the attacks, these victims also claim physical injury. But they were not able to file before the original fund's December 2003 statutory deadline because they did not manifest any physical injury at the time. Suffering from latent disease and illness in the ensuing years, they mounted a vigorous political lobbying effort. Asserting arguments of basic fairness, the first responders convinced Congress to reopen the fund to consider their claims.

In one real sense, therefore, reopening the 9/11 fund is simply designed to close the final chapter on compensating victims of the terrorist attacks. Sheila Birnbaum, a nationally recognized lawyer and expert in mass torts, was selected by the Department of Justice to serve as special master in designing and implementing the fund. Birnbaum had served as the court-appointed mediator in successfully resolving the ninety-four lawsuits brought by the 9/11 families who opted out of the original compensation program. Credible, a skilled negotiator, and sensitive to the needs of these families, she patiently worked to settle each and every one of the lawsuits pending in the federal court in Manhattan.

But in its rush to meet lame-duck deadlines before adjourning, Congress enacted a new law with unintended consequences. First, unlike the original statute, the new fund has a fixed appropriation of $4.2 billion, guaranteeing that many claimants will argue that they are being deliberately underpaid to make sure that funds are available for others. Second, the statute is not restricted to first responders; residents of lower Manhattan and elsewhere are, at least theoretically, eligible to apply for compensation. Nor are reasonable time or physical proximity limitations imposed on where or how soon a victim was exposed to harmful dust and debris. New Yorkers living on Staten Island, who were exposed to World Trade Center dust months after the attacks when construction vehicles began transporting debris to the Fresh Kills Landfill, might apply for compensation. Finally, the special master can surely expect that first responders who were paid by the original fund but in the past few years have developed more serious physical injuries, such as cancer, will apply for additional compensation. Further regulations will need to sort out all of these new problems.

There are subtle but important similarities between the Agent Orange payment program and the 9/11 fund. At first blush they are, of course, quite different: Agent Orange compensation followed from a judicially imposed settlement engineered by Judge Weinstein; the September 11th Victim Compensation Fund was authorized by Congress and duly signed into law by President George W. Bush. Relatively modest Agent Orange payments were made by eight chemical company defendants confronting the specter of protracted tort litigation; the 9/11 fund was composed entirely of public taxpayer funds, and the generosity of the payments was unprecedented.

Yet both Agent Orange and the 9/11 fund are prime examples of "bending the law" to meet immediate societal needs. Weinstein was determined to assist Vietnam veterans returning home from an unpopular war. With a unique compensation scheme, he sought to resolve a problem national in scope, historically lasting, and enormously painful. Similarly, Congress created a unique compensation scheme following one of the worst tragedies in American history. Not only was the 9/11 fund designed with the victims in mind; it also was a type of "vengeful philanthropy," showing the world (and the terrorists) that Americans were still united as one. Both Agent Orange and the 9/11 fund involved creative, unconventional thinking in the interest of advancing larger societal goals—unified community-wide political support for the victims, official evidence of the healing process involving both victims and the American people, the need to turn the page and move on while never forgetting the victims, and of course, financial aid to assist those in need.

Neither program will likely be repeated. But both demonstrate in real-life terms how the law can respond to meet threats confronting not only individual victims but American society as a whole.

— 4 —

THE HOKIE SPIRIT
MEMORIAL FUND

———

All Lives Have Equal Value

As we've seen, the tort system awards damages based on economic loss and pain and suffering. In one sense, this seems fair; the goal is to compensate for the measurable loss an individual or family experiences as a result of an unjust injury, thereby "making them whole" to the extent that money can do so. But in another sense this system feels unfair, violating core beliefs many of us share about the ultimate equality of all people. What about the argument that all lives should be valued the same, regardless of status or station? Can one design a credible, just compensation program in which the families of the waiter and the busboy receive the exact same payment as those of the stockbroker and the banker? Where is it written that the tort system, and the tort system alone, must be the guiding force in determining who gets what?

In allocating settlement proceeds in Agent Orange, the court operated under the shadow of a tort system that had triggered the class action lawsuit in the first place. And in establishing the September 11th Victim Compensation Fund, Congress expressly mandated that principles of tort law guide the special master's discretion. I was given wide latitude by the statute to adjust individual compensation awards to promote overall fairness. Nevertheless, traditional tort considerations of economic loss and pain and suffering were basic to my payment calculations. The statute required this.

But what if neither the courts nor the Congress had an official say in how one went about compensating the victims of tragedy? If constrained by neither legal precedent nor statutory language, how could a purely private compensation program be drafted to pay eligible claimants? The "who" and "what" of "who gets what?" could then be decided without reference to any binding instructions from government.

This is the situation I confronted in compensating the victims of the Virginia Tech shootings.

On April 16, 2007, on the campus of Virginia Tech, a state university in rural Blacksburg, Virginia, twenty-three-year-old student Seung-Hui Cho massacred twenty-seven students and five members of the school faculty in random acts of violence rarely seen in American history. Armed with chains, locks, a hammer, a knife, two handguns, and almost four hundred rounds of ammunition, Cho methodically conducted two separate attacks, two hours apart. The first two victims were killed in their West Ambler Hall residence at 7:15 A.M. Nearly two hours later, Cho chained the main entrances of Norris Hall, the venue for faculty offices, classrooms, and laboratories, and began chapter two of the carnage. He visited various classrooms at random, shut the doors, and sprayed the room with bullets, killing thirty and wounding twenty-three students who either were shot or were physically injured leaping from second-floor windows. As the police closed in, Cho killed himself.

In the immediate aftermath, school officials and campus police were criticized for failing to respond adequately to the initial shootings in West Ambler Hall, and for their delay in warning the campus community of the ongoing attacks. A subsequent investigation documented that the gunman had a long history of mental illness and in 2005 had actually been accused of stalking two female students. Declared mentally unfit by a Virginia court, he had been ordered to undergo mental health treatment. But, concerned about federal privacy laws and the rights of students, and hindered by the fact that the two women refused to press stalking charges, Virginia Tech had taken no further official action.

The shootings were, of course, national news. The media besieged the campus. The killings occupied newspaper front pages for weeks: stories about the gunman, acts of bravery and courage by the victims, the school's response to the shootings, the impact of the tragedy on surviving students and the campus community, and the future of Virginia Tech.

Meanwhile, unsolicited private contributions poured into the school, checks and cash ranging from pennies to a $1 million contribution from George Steinbrenner and the New York Yankees baseball team. About $8 million was contributed over the next few months, with checks made payable at random to Virginia Tech, "the Virginia Tech scholarship fund," "the Virginia Tech shootings," and other descriptive payees. Ultimately these monies found their way into a new Virginia Tech bank account called the Hokie Spirit Memorial Fund (named after the school mascot).

Officials at Virginia Tech had to decide how to distribute the money. Who would get what—and on what basis?

The tragedy had occurred on the watch of Charles Steger, the university's quiet, unassuming fifty-nine-year-old president. Steger exhibited all the characteristics of a typical university professor: thoughtful, unassuming, measured in word and deed, he seemed perfect for quiet, rural Blacksburg. Most at home with university budget issues, questions of faculty tenure, and the future of the Virginia Tech football team post–star quarterback Michael Vick, Steger was at sea when it came to the shootings. This was understandable. Nobody could have prepared him—or any other college president—for the daily news barrage that began with the first reports of the tragedy. First he had to respond to the immediacy of events on campus as Blacksburg was overwhelmed by TV camera trucks and reporters from national and local news outlets. Then, after the initial wave of attention subsided, he had to step back and decide an appropriate course of action for distributing millions of dollars of voluntary contributions received from concerned and empathetic citizens.

Virginia Tech was not in the claims compensation business. Its leadership had neither the experience nor the expertise to decide who got what. They needed help.

About two weeks after the shootings, I was in my Washington office when I received a call from Mary Ware of the Virginia Workers Compensation Commission. She quickly came to the point. President Steger and the university administration had absolutely no idea how to handle compensation issues for the dead and wounded. But they had followed my progress in designing and administering the September 11th Victim Compensation Fund. Perhaps my earlier work could help shape a payment program for the families and victims of the Virginia Tech shootings. A visit to the campus might be worthwhile. Would I come to Blacksburg to meet with Steger and his senior staff to discuss what might be done? The president would send a private university plane to ferry me to the remote campus.

I quickly agreed to make the trip. Within a few days I arrived at Virginia Tech (the first of a half dozen visits), where a towering 60,000-seat football stadium occupied center stage and overwhelmed the surrounding landscape. Blacksburg was more a village than a town, quiet and unassuming, with little traffic. I found its stillness conspicuous and eerie in light of why I was there. The background belied the horror of the moment. It was hard for me to fathom how and why a student could undertake such a rampage and conduct such mass slaughter, especially in such a bucolic setting—a painful reminder of the haphazard, unpredictable circumstances of life and death.

I met with a shaken Steger and his senior staff in a hushed administration conference room. Virginia Tech simply did not know what to do with the millions of dollars it had received from individuals and businesses. How should the university allocate funds among the victims and their families? Perhaps the university should return the money to the senders with an expression of appreciation from the president. If the university accepted the funds, what were the tax consequences to the school, the victims, and the contributors?

Compensation suggestions were varied, thoughtful—and troubling.

Steger suggested that the money be used to fund scholarships in the names of the dead students and faculty members. To Steger, this seemed the most appropriate use of the funds: "Ken, Virginia Tech is a university; scholarships will link the contributions to the school's mandate and reason for being. Something positive and permanent can yet result from the tragedy."

General Counsel Kay Heidbreder then offered her perspective: "Most of the dead were full-time students. But five faculty members also died, and they were wage earners. Shouldn't the families of the faculty receive more compensation than families of the students? This is what you did with the 9/11 fund. Economic loss might dictate awarding more compensation to employed faculty members than students on scholarship." To Heidbreder, familiar with both the tort system and the 9/11 fund, tort law might be the best benchmark for fashioning a Virginia Tech payment program.

Other university officials chimed in. Many around the table suggested placing limitations on how the families and injured victims could use the money: "We can't award money to a family that will accept it and then take a vacation to Disneyland to honor the life of a dead son or daughter," said one Steger aide.

And what about the students who were physically injured but survived? Should they be compensated? Some students escaped the horror by jumping out of second-floor windows and broke arms and legs. Other students suffered serious but nonfatal gunshot wounds. How would a compensation program make distinctions among the wounded?

Still other students had been in the classroom, witnessing the carnage firsthand, but through sheer luck and good fortune they lived to tell the tale. Now they suffered from post-traumatic stress disorder and other adverse mental conditions. Should they be paid? If so, what about the hundreds of other students who observed the events from their college dormitories or watched television at the Virginia Tech student union? Were they eligible for compensation?

During my initial visit, and over the course of several subsequent meetings in Blacksburg during the following weeks, I responded to all of these complex and thorny problems by offering Steger and his colleagues a primer on victim compensation. Steger and Heidbreder made every effort to be as hands-on as possible. They rarely left the room during hours of meetings, listening intently and scribbling notes while I laid out various compensation options. They obviously were being pressured from all sides—from victims and families seeking immediate compensation; from university officials worried about legal liability; from Virginia Tech's own lawyers questioning how private contributions made payable to the university could be used to compensate victims; and from the press, demanding to know whether and when money would be paid. I was impressed with both of them. They seemed driven by only one goal: to do the right thing with the limited funds available.

Gradually, over a period of less than one month, we managed to reach consensus around the conference table. After considering a number of options, the group, led by Steger and Heidbreder, was able to answer the tough questions. Virginia Tech was united in its approach.

Unlike the 9/11 fund, a limited amount of money was available in the Hokie Spirit Memorial Fund. To most people, $8 million might seem like a large sum. But paying thirty-two families of the dead, as well as scores of people who were physically injured or suffered mental disabilities after witnessing the attacks, would quickly deplete the fund and reduce amounts available to any individual victim.

This problem would be especially acute if economic loss became a prerequisite in calculating damages. Individual amounts would soar if the tort system was called into play. It would be a mistake. Limited funds needed to go a long way.

I also suggested that when it came to the families of the dead, all lives should be treated the same, whether those of students or faculty members. I urged the university not to replicate the 9/11 damage methodology (required by statute) of awarding different amounts to different individuals. They should allocate the same amount of money to those employed as to full-time students seeking a Virginia Tech diploma. As I told the university, "Why provoke a war among the thirty-two families as to who deserved what from a limited fund? In 9/11, the fireman's widow never understood why she was receiving millions of dollars less than the widow of the banker or stockbroker. We could avoid that problem with the Hokie Spirit Memorial Fund by implementing the notion that one size fits all.

Nor should the university impose any conditions on how eligible claimants could spend their awards. If a family wanted to visit Disneyland to honor the life of a son or daughter, why should Virginia Tech prevent it? If a vacation was unacceptable, what about buying a new car? Or investing in a business? Or paying for a second child's wedding? Who was to make such judgments? Compensating the families was, in effect, a "gift." No release would be required and no conditions whatsoever would be imposed preventing subsequent lawsuits. Any comparison to the 9/11 fund was, therefore, inapplicable. The families who accepted the money could turn around and use the funds to hire a lawyer to sue Virginia Tech if they so desired. The university would be merely distributing unsolicited private charitable donations to eligible claimants. If families wanted to sue the university, so be it.

President Steger pushed back a bit on this point, questioning whether a distinguished university should distribute limited funds for families potentially to take vacations or sue the university. But he gradually became comfortable with the idea of not restricting their use. Why second-guess emotional decisions made by families in grief? I again urged Virginia Tech to take a hands-off attitude: "Do not get into the business of challenging family decisions governing the funds they will receive. If you do so, you will find yourselves trapped, micromanaging subjective decisions by emotional, grieving families. Distance yourselves as much as possible from all of this. Authorize a check from the Hokie Spirit Memorial Fund and walk away."

Kay Heidbreder offered one reservation, pointing out that private individual contributors had designated a portion of the funds the university had received for a "Virginia Tech Scholarship Fund." I agreed with her that, in such cases, these contributions should be earmarked for scholarships to comply with donor intentions. Besides, only a few hundred thousand dollars of the total would be subject to this designation, an amount that would not have an appreciable effect on the overall distribution plan.

When it came to compensating the families of the victims, we all agreed that each family would receive the same amount: $208,000. This was a rather straightforward decision once we decided that all lives were of equal value. And most of the available funds—over $6.5 million distributed among the thirty-two families, out of approximately $7 million—would be allocated to pay these death claims. The remainder would be earmarked to deal with carefully defined physical injury and mental disability claims.

The university placed no limitations or restrictions on these awards; once the money was transferred to each family, they were free to dispose of the money without any university interference. In so doing, Virginia Tech expressly rejected the approach Congress took with the 9/11 fund. The university's program ignored the assumptions and methodology of the tort system.

What about the physically injured and those students suffering from mental trauma after witnessing the attacks? We quickly decided that those students who survived with gunshot wounds and broken bones should be compensated. But I again warned school officials to avoid becoming enmeshed in the claims processing business; in particular, I painted a parade of horrible possibilities, with school doctors and nurses spending days poring over detailed medical records, trying to determine the severity of physical injuries and the prioritization of claims of pain and suffering: "The school has neither the time nor the expertise to determine a hierarchy of physical injury claims," I said. "You want to avoid a situation where those physically injured can challenge the subjective discretion exercised by school medical personnel in deciding which injuries are more serious than others."

I offered a better way. Immediately after the shootings, physically injured students had been rushed to local hospitals, where they received emergency medical treatment. Some were treated and released; the more seriously injured were admitted and remained hospitalized for days, weeks, or even months. I proposed that hospitalization be an objective surrogate for pain and suffering. The longer the shooting victim remained in the hospital, the more likely the seriousness of the physical injury. A student who received outpatient medical treatment would receive much less compensation than a gunshot victim hospitalized for months. A simple, objective determination grounded in the length of a hospital stay would prioritize the allocation of dollars from the Hokie Spirit Memorial Fund.

School officials accepted this approach, quickly recognizing that it would avoid extensive wrangling among victims concerning whose injury was more serious when it came to compensation. For ease of administration, we created three objective tiers of physical injury compensation in the Virginia Tech Victim Assistance Program final protocol:

- A cash payment of $90,000 and a waiver of all "tuition and mandatory fees at Virginia Tech for the remainder of the claimants' current program of study" for physically injured students who were required to be hospitalized for at least ten days and nights
- A cash payment of $40,000 and a similar waiver of tuition and mandatory fees for those students hospitalized for three to nine days and nights

- A choice for students hospitalized for fewer than three days: a waiver of tuition and mandatory fees, or a cash payment of $10,000

The claims administrator would simply review hospital records to determine which category was relevant to a particular victim. End of analysis. No examination of medical records, nature of wounds, varying degrees of pain, short- or long-term disability, or other medical variables. Instead the administrator would use a single finding: how long the victim was hospitalized. This finding would determine the amount of compensation.

Similarly, the university needed to devise objective criteria—easily verifiable—to handle victim claims of mental trauma and disability. I reminded President Steger that we were entering uncharted seas, since the 9/11 statute had expressly prohibited such claims. We anguished over whether it made sense, in light of the limited amounts available in the Hokie Spirit Memorial Fund, to compensate such claims at all. We might receive thousands of these claims, not only from students bearing witness to the tragedy from their campus dormitory rooms but also from thousands or even millions of other observers watching events unfold on television and now claiming mental injury as a result. Like Congress, we had to take into account the possibility—the likelihood—of a flood of claims that would threaten to overwhelm claims administrators and exhaust the fund.

But the problem was more complicated. What about those students who were actually in the very classrooms where the gunman began shooting at random, killing fellow students while others escaped through pure chance or luck? In examining the evidence of that day, I was amazed at the stories I heard: how one victim died while another escaped because of the gunman's bad aim; how one student survived the murder spree by escaping while the gunman reloaded his weapons; the students in the classroom who jumped to safety from a second-floor window, hid under a desk, or faked death. These students certainly had legitimate mental injury claims. I shuddered to think about the short- and long-term mental impact of being a firsthand witness to such horror.

In any compensation program, mental injury claims raise a particularly sticky issue. The process of defining some claims as eligible while rejecting others is fraught with difficulty. It can be nearly impossible to objectively verify such claims. But beyond this problem of proof is the stark reality that the potential volume of claims can quickly outstrip limited financial resources. The only solution is to carefully restrict eligibility for compensation.

To create a formula that would pay legitimate mental injury claims of students who witnessed the carnage firsthand, while denying the claims of all others, we devised a physical proximity test, an attempt to avoid an influx of mental distress claims from a national TV audience. The final protocol spelled out the distinction:

This category of [mental injury] claimants includes all individuals who were present in Norris Hall Classroom Nos. 204, 205, 206, 207, and 211 where the shootings occurred on April 16, 2007, and are not covered under any of the categories listed above. Each of these claimants will be eligible for tuition and mandatory fees for the remainder of the claimant's current program of study at Virginia Tech (i.e., undergraduate or graduate degree program enrolled in on August 20, 2007) as long as the claimant remains a student in good standing making satisfactory progress toward that degree and the enrollment in the program of study is continuous. (The value of the tuition and fees may not be converted to a cash payment.) In lieu of the tuition and fees, the claimant may select a cash payment of $10,000.

We also had to draft a map to determine eligibility. There was no practical alternative. We could not rely upon the expert medical opinions of psychiatrists or psychologists; the medical profession could not solve our dilemma and would delay the prompt distribution of money. We could not wade through hundreds of pages of medical documents and learned opinion. Instead we drew some important intuitive conclusions. The closer the claimant was to the tragedy—in the classrooms, in the line of fire, avoiding death by good luck and good fortune—the more likely the possibility of mental injury. "Rough justice" indeed. But a realistic solution to a complex and thorny problem.

Once the compensation program was finalized, Steger asked me to act as administrator of the Hokie Spirit Memorial Fund. He suggested that distributing the funds might be a relatively simple task: "Ken, this is not like the September 11th Victim Compensation Fund. There is a modest amount of money to be distributed to a limited number of people; it should not take too much of your time."

I accepted the assignment, working pro bono because of the limited funds. Just as had been the case with the 9/11 fund, I did not think it appropriate to demand a fee for my legal services when the perpetrator of the tragedy was dead and the community was enveloped by grief. I did not want to be perceived as profiting from the shootings. But I warned Steger that administering the fund—even though the compensation would be deemed a gift to a limited number of eligible claimants—would take more time than he had predicted: "Do not underestimate the challenge; families will be skeptical, emotional, and in many cases angry and frustrated. They will view the fund as 'hush money,' an attempt by Virginia Tech to placate their anger with money, an attempt to 'buy off' lawsuits."

To address this concern, I decided to meet with any family or injured victim who wanted to be heard. Confidential, private hearings had worked well in administering the 9/11 fund, and offering this opportunity to all claimants would go a long way in encouraging participation in the fund.

I scheduled private individual meetings on the Virginia Tech campus, as well as in northern Virginia and even Trenton, New Jersey, where a few of the families lived. The hearings were not mandatory, and fewer than half of the eligible claimants took advantage of the opportunity (approximately the same percentage that requested a 9/11 fund hearing). Each hearing lasted about thirty minutes. As I had expected, some claimants welcomed the opportunity to vent about life's unfairness, to validate the memory of a lost loved one, or to relive, moment by moment, the tragedy they witnessed in Norris Hall. It was not about the compensation, which had already been determined in the final protocol; instead it was about providing people the chance to bare their souls, articulating in often eloquent language their effort to come to grips with a life suddenly pushed off the rails by an unfathomable, unpredictable tragedy. Many focused almost exclusively on the personality and character of the victim or how the family would attempt to cope with the sudden loss of the family's shining light. Family after family commented on the void created by the sudden loss of a child or a sibling. Often the claimant would seem to be talking to himself or herself, softly uttering words without seeming to recognize that I was even in the room:

> My daughter was going to go to medical school after graduation. What a doctor she would have been. She always wanted to help others.

> My son loved Virginia Tech and attended all the football games. Sometimes I think that's why he selected Virginia Tech. I don't understand how this could happen. Why him? Why now? Why here? I don't understand. I don't understand.

A few of the claimants asked pointed questions about the final protocol and our method of determining who got what:

> Mr. Feinberg, why doesn't your formula recognize that my spouse, who died in Norris Hall, was a wage earner, a member of the faculty earning an annual salary? Shouldn't the formula distinguish between those employed and those students who were on scholarship and were not bringing home a paycheck each week?

I explained that there was not enough money available to make such distinctions and that, in any event, unlike the 9/11 fund, the Hokie Spirit Memorial Fund was in no way tied to the tort system. The claimant could receive compensation and then turn around and file a lawsuit against Virginia Tech. The courtroom would recognize such an important tort distinction; this fund could not.

Another parent voiced a different concern:

> My son was seriously wounded by the gunman. He was rushed to the hospital. When the doctors suggested that he be admitted for medical treatment, he refused, making it clear that he wanted to return to his dormitory to be with his friends. Your physical injury compensation formula depends upon the number of days the victim is in a hospital. Why? My son should not be punished because of his courage and fortitude in refusing to be admitted. He should be treated as if he had been hospitalized for a week or more.

I explained that the physical injury compensation formula needed to be administered in an objective and efficient manner. Subjective considerations of courage or fortitude could not possibly be accepted without hopelessly complicating the determination of payments. Philosophers, psychiatrists, and priests might factor courage into the equation; I could not.

The Virginia Tech hearings confirmed a few important lessons I learned over the years about designing and administering compensation systems—lessons that may apply, in some form, to any attempt to create a process to encourage healing after a terrible tragedy.

First, do not underestimate the importance of providing grieving claimants the opportunity to be heard in a confidential face-to-face meeting. In Agent Orange, the September 11th Victim Compensation Fund, and the Hokie Spirit Memorial Fund, substance was often trumped by procedure, the calculation of damages less important than the claimants' desire to speak about the victim with the person making compensation decisions and to express their grief over the unfair, arbitrary actions of human beings that affect both the living and the dead. The medium was as important, maybe even more so, than the message.

But the volume of claims makes a difference. Obviously, the fewer the claimants, the easier it is to provide a tailored individual opportunity to meet with the claims administrator. In my administration of the 9/11 fund and the Hokie Spirit Memorial Fund, the relatively modest number of claimants enabled us to make the right to be heard a fundamental pillar of these compensation programs. But as claim volume increases, individual hearings become less and less practical. The twin goals of efficiency and speed can be fatally undercut if the number of hearings threatens to clog the system. In designing an effective compensation program aimed at determining who gets what, an administrator wants to encourage as many eligible claimants as possible to enter the system. But in such cases, one pays a heavy price for success; claims volume diminishes personal, one-on-one treatment with claimants, and the impersonal and bureaucratic replace the intimacy of a more modest program, where claimants believe they are not simply consumers of assembly-line justice. Ironically, the greater the number of claimants who feel comfortable with a compensation system and actively want to participate, the greater the threat posed by the sheer magnitude of the claims, at least when it comes to their believing that they are being treated as individuals in a fair and consistent manner.

Finally, the Hokie Spirit Memorial Fund provides important evidence concerning the effect of a compensation system on those claimants who retain the right to sue in court. Even though all two hundred eligible claimants who received compensation had every right to use the money to hire a lawyer and file a lawsuit against Virginia Tech, only two chose to do so (and would eventually win a courtroom victory against the university). All the other claimants accepted the amounts they received from the fund as their total compensation from Virginia Tech.

There are various reasons for this. Virginia law caps individual tort damages against a state university, such as Virginia Tech, at $100,000 per victim, thereby discouraging would-be litigants from seeking a pot of gold in the courtroom. In addition, Virginia Tech undoubtedly planned to mount a vigorous defense against allegations that it had been negligent and could have prevented the killings. Who could reasonably have foreseen that a deranged student would arm himself to the teeth and initiate a killing spree on the rural Blacksburg campus? And, of course, any trial and subsequent appeals would take years before a final judgment would be rendered.

But I believe there is an additional reason lawsuits directed at Virginia Tech were so rare: the emotional impact of the Hokie Spirit Memorial Fund itself. The fund evidenced a collective empathy, a compassion and sensitivity on the part of the Virginia Tech family and surrounding Blacksburg. In effect, it was Virginia Tech saying to the victims, "We are with you in spirit." It is much easier to recognize this sense of community in a rural college setting such as Blacksburg. Unlike New York City or Washington, D.C., people are more likely to know their neighbors, to be part of a college campus. They bear some allegiance not only to students and faculty but just as important, to Virginia Tech itself. The school's shadow hovers over Blacksburg and its citizens.

The importance of this communitarian feeling cannot be overstated. In hearing after hearing, grieving families and injured victims expressed their support and profound respect for the greater Virginia Tech community. Many claimants offered gratitude for the funds and thanked me for offering compensation without any preconditions. Almost all concluded that Virginia Tech had treated them fairly and had demonstrated its compassion and sensitivity toward the victims. The university had tried to do the right thing by distributing modest available compensation fairly and equitably. It had come to the rescue.

The Virginia Tech story has important implications for policy makers considering similar compensation programs in the future. As we've seen, the 9/11 fund was tied in part to the tort system. Victims were required to agree not to sue before receiving compensation. To induce them to do so, compensation amounts were deliberately linked to tort-system considerations such as lost income—which forced me to take on the almost impossible task of assigning a fair value to each life lost. The initial determinations triggered misunderstanding, resentment, and bitterness. It took me months to repair the damage.

By contrast, the Virginia Tech payments, untethered to the tort system, were pure gifts—evidence of citizen compassion. This meant that the sums paid to each victim or family could be the same, which not only simplified the process but, more important, also appealed to the deeply ingrained American value that "all men are created equal." As a result, lawsuits were largely avoided even without requiring a formal promise not to sue.

The lesson: how victims perceive community reaction to their plight and how we go about determining who gets what can prove essential in convincing such victims not to sue. Valuing lives equally also creates a quicker, surer, more profound sense of healing for the entire community.

–5–

PAYING WALL STREET
EXECUTIVES

"I Believe in You"

Until June 2009, my professional role in determining who gets what involved calculating damages for victims of tragedy: Vietnam veterans exposed to Agent Orange, innocent bystanders of the 9/11 terrorist attacks, and students and faculty murdered by a student misfit at Virginia Tech. In an emotionally charged atmosphere characterized by grief, frustration, and anger, my role was to determine the value of life itself and to find a way to offer solace to those suffering loss and disability through no fault of their own. I was immersed in a strange, surreal world where I was required to apply a dollar figure to every victim.

However, in one sense my work—though unique—was tied at least in some way to the prevailing legal system, where judges and juries determine liability and calculate damage awards every day in courts throughout the nation, guided by tort law and the concept of compensation paid to innocent victims in recognition of their loss. Then, after the shock of the 2008 financial crisis, the trajectory of my career changed course.

Treasury Secretary Timothy Geithner asked me to undertake a new public service assignment with no historical parallel—this time to determine pay packages for selected members of the business elite. My role would be to analyze all the facts and figures surrounding corporate pay and calculate *in specific dollars* what a chief executive officer or chief financial officer should earn. It would be an entirely new and controversial variation on the familiar question of who gets what.

The justification for my new role could be traced directly to Congress.

Compelled to use taxpayer dollars to bail out American companies on the verge of bankruptcy—a blue-chip list that included Citigroup, Bank of America, and the insurance giant American International Group (AIG)—Congress could not stand idly by and accept a one-way bargain with Wall Street. There would have to be a price to pay for such congressional largesse. Constituents would be appalled at the idea of Congress using public funds to rescue private companies headed by corporate chieftains earning millions of dollars. The political problem was especially acute during a time of growing unemployment, widespread hardship, and financial uncertainty. The politics of the bailout demanded that we impose penalties. The Emergency Economic Stabilization Act of 2008, which created the Trouble Asset Relief Program (TARP), authorized the Treasury secretary to use public funds "to promote financial market stability." Pursuant to this new statute, the Treasury Department in both the Bush and Obama administrations propped up corporate

America by purchasing company shares of stock worth trillions of dollars. These purchases—in the form of loans that the government hoped would one day be repaid—were a first. In effect, the American taxpayer now owned a majority equity stake in some of the largest American businesses in financial distress.

At the same time, Congress passed the American Recovery and Reinvestment Act (ARRA) of 2009, which imposed new restrictions and requirements on paying corporate executives at the individual companies receiving the most TARP financial assistance: AIG, Bank of America, Citigroup, Chrysler, Chrysler Financial, General Motors, and GMAC. When it came to these seven companies—and only these seven—Treasury would have a pervasive role: determining the specific compensation packages for each of the top twenty-five officials of these companies. The CEOs, CFOs, senior vice presidents, and top Wall Street traders would submit to having their pay fixed directly by the government. In addition, Treasury would promulgate rules and regulations governing how each of these corporations would go about compensating its next seventy-five senior officials. The government also would have veto power over the proposed compensation structures.

If Main Street was required to come to Wall Street's rescue, there would be a price to pay: leaders in Congress and the new Obama administration didn't want to see headlines describing how financial "fat cats" were collecting outrageous salaries from companies supported by taxes on ordinary citizens.

This one-of-a-kind statute placed the Treasury Department squarely in the compensation business. Treasury—not the companies themselves—would now decide the appropriateness of private corporate pay.

ARRA made it clear that until and unless each corporation re-paid all of its debt to the taxpayers, compensation restrictions would continue to apply. Specific statutory language also prohib-ited compensation that would encourage senior corporate officers from taking unnecessary and excessive risks in the marketplace, and any corporate bonus or other incentive compensation would have to be paid in the form of long-term restricted stock that could not fully vest or be redeemable as long as the corporation still owed money to the taxpayers. Treasury could also seek to recover, or "clawback," from the corporation previously paid incentive com-pensation. And "golden parachute" payments—overly generous guaranteed severance payments to departing corporate officials— were prohibited. The new statute required that Treasury issue addi-tional regulations defining in more detail how it would implement these directives. The creation of these rules was motivated by sev-eral impulses. One was the traditional "good government" concern over prudent use of taxpayer dollars. It would seem inappropriate for TARP government funds to be used to subsidize payments in the hundreds of millions of dollars to individual financial execu-tives, particularly in a time of economic hardship for so many Americans. Members of Congress, senators, even presidents don't earn paychecks like that—why should anyone dependent on pub-lic funds be compensated in such a fashion?

A second was the desire not to reward excessive risk-taking by corporate managers. With the global financial system having nearly collapsed partly as a result of overly risky bets by executives eager to boost profits and thereby increase their own bonuses, many experts felt it was important to begin reforming the incen-tive system that governed financial decision-making. The compensation paid to bankers and others bailed out by TARP seemed a natural place to start.

The third driving factor—perhaps the most diffuse and ill-defined, yet potentially the most explosive—was voter anger over the perceived misdeeds of the financial community and the populist demand that Wall Street's "fat cats" ought to pay a price for their crimes.

American history documents time and again the ongoing tension between Main Street and Wall Street: Hamilton versus Jefferson; the nineteenth-century Jacksonian political struggle over a national bank; the tycoons of the Gilded Age versus the Progressive movement; and the political battles over Roosevelt's New Deal. But Congress had gone further than ever before. With excessive corporate pay the sore point and heedless Wall Street executives the culprits, Congress would directly intervene and require that the government determine the private compensation of those responsible for the financial debacle. No question: this was a first.

But somebody had to make these compensation determinations. The new statute delegated the responsibility to the secretary of the Treasury. But Congress well knew that Treasury Secretary Geithner would have neither the time nor the political inclination to weigh in on a subject as contentious and problematic as regulating private corporate pay. Besides, the Department of the Treasury—the bastion and symbol of the free market system, of capitalism itself—was not in the business of micromanaging private business compensation decisions as to who gets what.

A few weeks after President Barack Obama signed the legislation into law, I received a call from Neal Wolin, the deputy secretary and number-two man at Treasury. A forty-seven-year-old former wunderkind with a pedigree that included Yale Law School and stints as head of a Hartford Insurance division and deputy White House counsel, Wolin was a solid public servant who combined enormous competence with political acumen and creativity. Over the years Wolin and I had worked together in a vain attempt to solve the national asbestos litigation crisis that threatened to overwhelm the courts.

Wolin quickly came to the point: "Ken, have you read the new statute requiring the secretary to fix corporate pay? We need to create Treasury regulations implementing the statute. Do you have any ideas? Can you help?" He then threw in the kicker: "Do you have any interest in taking on the job?" Treasury needed to distance itself as much as possible from the day-to-day role of fixing corporate pay. Was I available?

Happy to help the Obama administration and take up the challenge of a new public assignment, I told Wolin yes. I seconded his opinion that it made political sense for the secretary to delegate his authority under the statute to an official who would not be part of the Treasury bureaucracy. I suggested appointing a special master according to Treasury regulations. This new official—not Geithner—would design and administer the new compensation program. The political heat would be directed at the special master.

Wolin was now reading from a well-prepared script. He had the entire plan worked out in his mind before he even called me. Now that I had expressed interest, he deferred any further action until he formally advanced his idea with the secretary and others at Treasury and the White House. With me in the fold, a specific point man willing and able to act as special master, he now had the ammunition needed to sell his idea. He anticipated that any appointment would promote controversy from red-state Republicans in Congress who rejected the idea of big government fixing private corporate compensation, but also from blue-state Democrats who would howl if the pay determinations did not adequately reflect populist outrage toward Wall Street.

It looked like a lose-lose situation. "But you relish controversy," Wolin observed. "You won't mind this latest blowup."

A few days later Wolin called again, informing me that his plan was moving forward and that I should schedule an appointment with Geithner. I met with the secretary, Wolin, Treasury adviser Gene Sperling, and a few other members of the senior staff in the secretary's impressive, carpeted Treasury office overlooking the Washington Mall. The secretary thanked me for my willingness to consider the assignment, raising his eyebrows at the very idea of such a statute. He was all business. I was impressed with his knowledge of the statute. He was thoroughly familiar with the language of the new law and the conflicting obligations it imposed on the Department of the Treasury (and on him personally). He immediately expressed reservations about the Treasury Department's role in fixing private corporate pay.

But our conversation quickly evolved from the theoretical to the practical. He reminded me that the taxpayers had loaned the seven companies billions of dollars, money still very much at risk in an uncertain financial environment. He expressed concern that Main Street anger directed at corporate pay could further jeopardize these companies' already tottering financial stability. Responsible for the safety and security of the nation's financial system, the secretary had little interest in promoting excessively

harsh compensation policies that could further weaken the damaged economy.

The secretary made clear that my primary goal as Treasury's
special master for TARP executive compensation was to determine payments for senior corporate officials that would maxi-
mize the likelihood that the designated companies would repay
TARP loans as quickly as possible. The taxpayers had to be made
whole. This was the top priority—not any effort to "punish" corporate officials by cutting their pay to rock bottom or any attempt to placate congressional critics saddling up to pit Main
Street against Wall Street.

Sperling's take was all political. He saw the statute as a mischievous attempt by Congress to inject politics into the complexities of determining private corporate pay. He warned that I would
be buffeted by conflicting political pressures: congressional Republicans having second thoughts about the statute; Democrats
demanding that Treasury slash corporate pay closer to the bone. I
agreed with him. I perceived nothing but political trouble arising
out of the statutory directive to the secretary of the Treasury.

If the secretary came across as careful, studied, and deliberate,
Sperling was a frenetic whirlwind, his mind racing from one political consequence to another. Together the two of them provided
me an excellent preview of what was to come.

Whatever could be done to satisfy the statute (and congressional
critics) by reducing compensation excesses should be encouraged;
the law and politics required it. But not at the risk of driving these
seven companies into defaulting on their financial obligations to
the American taxpayer. The secretary was clear on this fundamental point.

Wolin's plan had worked. The secretary offered me the job and I agreed to work, again, without compensation as a special Treasury employee. He expressed his total support for my effort in implementing these seemingly conflicting objectives. I would be as independent and free from Treasury interference as the statute and regulations would allow. The Office of the Special Master for TARP Executive Compensation technically would be housed in Treasury's Office of Financial Stability, headed by the former president and CEO of Merrill Lynch, Herb Allison. But in reality I would look to Neal Wolin—the architect of the entire plan—to resolve any intramural policy disputes that might arise. As for the secretary, I would meet with him only two or three times during my sixteen-month tenure as special master.

I now confronted the task of assembling a first-rate team of lawyers, experts in executive compensation, and support personnel to occupy the special master's office in the basement of the main Treasury building. But this was easy. I knew I could count on two loyal colleagues from my law firm: Camille Biros and Jacqueline Zins, who had been part of my law practice for decades. Both of them had been at my side during my administration of the 9/11 fund. When I learned that career Treasury officials were also available and eager to assist in implementing the new program, I took advantage.

Twelve Treasury professionals were assigned to my office. The TARP companies quickly learned that they were up against a formidable group; they could not prevail with bluster and sophistry. Arguments about compensation would be decided on merit, based upon the evidence submitted and the policy decisions made. The Department of the Treasury would be more than equal to the task.

I also wanted to retain a few private executive compensation experts, not only to assist in the substantive task of determining appropriate corporate pay, but also to blunt the criticism that was sure to come: that Feinberg and Treasury simply didn't understand the Wall Street corporate culture and the competitive environment when it came to pay. What better way to weather the gathering storm than by hiring consultants actually working the Wall Street beat.

But I soon discovered that it was all but impossible to find credible, truly independent commercial compensation consultants. All the major consulting firms specializing in executive compensation suffered from the same problem: a real or perceived conflict of interest in representing the very types of companies and corporate officials subject to my new regulatory authority. I was already learning a valuable lesson even before I began my work. In making pay decisions, American businesses and their favorite "independent" compensation consultants worked hand in glove, comparing notes and sizing up the competition. Under the guise of promoting "competitive pay practices," true independence became diluted as consultants recommended increasing pay for their corporate clients as a way to ingratiate themselves with the executives who'd hired them in the first place. Their very livelihood was a self-fulfilling prophecy.

At least this was the perception. And in the politically charged world of Washington, perception was reality.

So I did the next best thing: I retained the services of two academics, experts in the field, professors Lucian Bebchuk of Harvard Law School and Kevin Murphy of the University of Southern California. Both were accomplished scholars who had very different worldviews of compensation. Bebchuk believed the government should intervene, while Murphy felt it should maintain a hands-off free market attitude. As the special master, I would cite their input, not only to buttress the credibility of our compensation determinations but also, just as important, to secure some additional political cover: "the two nationally recognized professors signed off on what we are doing."

TARP Compensation Treasury Regulations would spell out the variables to consider in determining who got what. Building on the new statute, the regulations focused on seven guiding principles that would put big business on notice when it came to pay:

1. *Risk.* Compensation packages should avoid incentives that encourage corporate executives to take "excessive" risks that threaten the financial viability of the company. Risk is not to be discouraged; it is an integral part of our free market system. But "excessive" risk—whatever that means—is something else again. This concern about risk—the idea that compensation practices all too often reflect and encourage greedy corporate behavior—was, of course, a populist favorite underlying the new statute.

2. *Taxpayer return.* This was Secretary Geithner's primary concern. Compensation should reflect the need for the company to recruit and retain key employees so the company ultimately could repay every cent borrowed. Pay back the taxpayers— with interest. Every company subject to my jurisdiction, and much of the Treasury bureaucracy, referenced this variable in urging the special master to be generous when it came to compensation.

3. *Different types of compensation.* Corporate pay packages should be diverse, a mix of base salary and incentives, including cash, stock, executive pensions, and other monetary benefits. "Golden parachutes" are prohibited by statute; all other financial benefits are subject to review by the special master.

4. *Performance-based compensation.* This is the heart and soul of the regulations, a direct response to congressional outrage. Only an executive's base salary is guaranteed. The remainder of the compensation package depends on individual and corporate performance over at least three years. Short-term corporate success should not trigger additional compensation; instead the regulations focus on extended corporate growth. Corporate officials and the companies they manage should be joined at the hip when it comes to compensation.

5. *Relating to the competition.* Companies must be able to compete in the marketplace. Accordingly, the pay packages the special master reviews and approves should be competitive with those of other businesses. Placing these distressed companies at a competitive disadvantage is self-defeating; the goal is to restore them to health, not inflict additional chronic pain by limiting pay. This was another variable corporate advocates constantly cited in pushing back on the special master's findings.

6. *Focusing on the individual.* Both the compensation structures and amounts paid to each corporate official should reflect the individual's current and prospective contributions to the company's overall value. Obvious, perhaps, except that the regulations delineate examples of these "contribu-

tions," for example, revenue production, specific expertise, compliance with company policy, and corporate leadership. In sum, what role did the corporate official play with respect to changes in the company's financial health or competitive position?

7. *Discretion.* Finally, the regulations delegate to the special master broad discretion to determine the appropriate weight or relevance to give these various compensation principles, depending upon the facts and circumstances of each case.

As with my administration of the September 11th Victim Compensation Fund, both the statute and the regulations conferred a huge amount of discretion on one person with ultimate responsibility to determine who got what. It is this discretion—largely free of other governmental checks and balances—that led the media to confer the title of "pay czar" on the new special master. Although I chuckled at how confused my grandfather from Lithuania would have been to learn that his grandson had become a "czar," I disliked the term. I was not a czar issuing arbitrary imperial decrees about pay based upon whim or fancy. The statute and accompanying regulations were clear in defining the authority of the Treasury Department and went even further, detailing the specific factors to be considered in calculating executive pay. I could not roam at will exercising unfettered discretion. Far from being some type of "czar," I was trying to walk the line between populist sentiment and the legitimate concerns that pay be tied to performance and that these seven companies repay the taxpayer. This was a fine line indeed. I was a mediator, not a czar, balancing competing public policy interests in an effort to comply with a hastily written,

politically charged statute. But the title "pay czar" would dog me
throughout my tenure.

The tension inherent in my assignment would only increase in
the ensuing months. I took heat not just from the seven companies
under my purview but also from Treasury officials themselves—especially Herb Allison and Tim Massad in the Office of Financial
Stability, and Jim Milstein, who was responsible for Treasury oversight of AIG. He continually complained to Wolin that my effort
to rein in corporate compensation packages threatened to undercut
their efforts at restoring financial stability to companies on the
brink of ruin. They made excellent arguments. But I was determined to make an impact, and Wolin backed me up (while warning me to be careful with my brinksmanship). How far could I go
in complying with the statute and regulations? I needed to satisfy
a Congress reflecting Main Street anger while at the same time
making sure the seven companies would remain in business and
begin the torturous road back to financial health so the taxpayers
would be repaid. This was the challenge embedded in conflicting
public policy and political considerations.

I braced myself for attacks from both right and left. I assumed
that from ideological Republicans would come the argument that
the government, in the person of the pay czar, was interfering with
the free marketplace and laissez-faire capitalism, that private pay
was none of Treasury's business. Meanwhile, the Democrats would
blast my pay determinations as "too little, too late," that I was
merely a shill for corporate America. I told my Treasury team to
circle the wagons.

But the onslaught never came. I misread the congressional
mood. It had been Congress, after all, that enacted the statute au-

thorizing a limited government role in determining who got what. My jurisdiction was confined to the top twenty-five corporate officials in seven companies, a total of 175 individuals. I was presiding over a largely symbolic sideshow. This became apparent when I visited Senator Richard Shelby of Alabama, the ranking Republican on the Senate Banking Committee. "Ken," he told me, "you will have no trouble with me. I voted against TARP. I thought it was a mistake to use taxpayer money to save these companies. Now we are creditors and I believe that creditors have a right to fix corporate pay. Just don't expand your authority. Don't go beyond these seven companies. I won't object."

Camille Biros and I went to see Democratic Congressman Barney Frank, a key player in the House. He was blunt: "I'm focusing on the Dodd/Frank legislation, policies of the Federal Reserve, the SEC, and FDIC. Real changes in corporate pay won't come from your work; we need real, fundamental reform, and you are not it." Clearly if I did not attempt to broaden my mandate, and as long as Congress was preoccupied with other more pervasive and long-lasting financial regulatory reform initiatives, I would be left alone. I would receive a political pass.

Whatever the substantive merits of the statute mandating Treasury intervention in private corporate pay decisions, it quickly became clear to me that, at least politically, I could accomplish my mission by exercising narrow discretion and limiting the scope of my pay decisions. Do what Congress demanded; nothing more, nothing less.

Although Congress might not view my work as a top priority, the American people were eager, to a surprising degree, to see exactly how I would answer the question of who gets what. I thought that determining pay for just 175 corporate officials would not be front-page news. I was wrong. In a time of great public uncertainty following the financial crisis and home mortgage debacle, with unemployment increasing and the gap widening between Wall Street and most other pay, the American people were very interested in exactly what dollars would be placed next to the name of a corporate master of the universe. What was a CEO at AIG or Bank of America worth? How much money should be paid the head of General Motors, currently exiting from bankruptcy? And what about the chief financial officer at Citigroup or AIG? These companies had driven themselves to the financial precipice, to the brink of ruin. What was appropriate pay—in actual specific dollars—for the individuals responsible? The taxpayers were eager to know the results; many were ready to criticize if the compensation packages were "excessive."

We began our work by providing each of the companies with a twenty-two-page, single-spaced set of instructions requesting extensive company and employee information, the compensation history of the top twenty-five corporate officials at the company, and competitive market data. In addition, we asked key questions: What did the company propose in the way of compensation, and what would be the suggested mix of such compensation keeping the statute and regulations in mind; for example, cash versus stock, base salary, short-term versus long-term pay, bonus payments, etc.? We asked the companies to lead with their chins: "You tell us what each official is worth."

Reams of paper flowed in from the companies. Many of them retained their own outside compensation experts and business consulting firms to advance their cause. The companies spent millions of dollars to prepare their submissions, which often were accompanied by colorful graphs and charts, a visual attempt to highlight the unique qualities of their key employees. Everyone was deemed "irreplaceable" and "essential," and the submissions all ended with the same bottom-line argument: "If you fix pay that is too low, our key people will leave the company and the taxpayers' TARP loans will be at risk. We are on the edge trying to survive; do not push us over the cliff." Occasionally a company would invoke the ultimate horror: departing employees would not simply depart for a more generous domestic competitor but would leave America altogether and go to work for a competing bank or auto company in Europe, Japan, or even China.

The submissions made it bold and stark—the special master's office held the future of the seven companies in its hands. So, Mr. Feinberg, you'd better be careful with your pay determinations.

The completed questionnaires and submissions were just the beginning of our process. We also collected information from our own independent sources (such as Equilar's Benchmark Top 25 Executive Compensation Benchmarking Pay report) in an effort to produce a more balanced, less argumentative picture of a company's pay practices in relation to the rest of the industry. We compared notes, placing our own data next to the statistics the companies submitted. Our two compensation experts also weighed in.

But the most important part of the process was the personal meetings we scheduled with company officials who sought an audience to plead their case on behalf of their key corporate employees. My previous experiences in determining who got what had taught me the value of face-to-face dialogue. Private, confidential meetings not only gave the participants an opportunity to make their arguments in person but also promoted a sense of due process and fairness. The special master would not make critically important compensation determinations based strictly on numbers, charts, and graphs. Instead every company had the right to be heard, to make the case, to influence the result.

The hearings helped to validate the entire compensation process by promoting its credibility. In participating in a private hearing, traveling to Washington to sit across the table from the special master and plead their case, company officials had a personal stake in the venture. They were directly co-opted into the process. Compensation determinations were not being made solely by pencil-pushing government functionaries in some dark basement office at Treasury; they were the result of a deliberative transparent process in which high-level company representatives themselves had a voice.

CEOs and their lawyers all traveled to Washington to mount the soapbox, warning about adverse consequences if pay demands were not met. It was not just the company and the taxpayers' money that were at risk; the American economy would suffer if particular officials did not get their due. The world was watching.

Two ground rules characterized these meetings. First, unless specifically requested, I would not meet with the 175 individual corporate officials who were the subjects of my pay determinations. Neither the statute nor the regulations contemplated this. I was engaged in a company-wide project focused on each company's compensation culture, and how designated officials in that company hierarchy were part of that culture. So when I met with CEOs, chief financial officers, and vice presidents of human resources, they came to see me wearing their official company hats, not to make self-serving arguments about their own individual pay.

Second, all sessions were conducted at the main Treasury building in Washington. As an experienced mediator, I knew the importance of conducting meetings in the most effective venue. The majesty and grandeur of this building, next door to the White House, offered me distinct advantages. Lavish and imposing, with oil paintings of previous Treasury secretaries lining the hallways and marble floors leading to plush conference rooms exhibiting antique desks and tables, this was the perfect forum to conduct hearings about pay. If not exactly intimidated by the surroundings, corporate officials immediately realized that they were up against a formidable negotiating partner—the federal government.

I explained that the special master was not an adversary, that I rejected the phrase "pay czar." Rather, I was a mediator hoping to achieve consensus pertaining to pay. But ultimately both the statute and the regulations conferred final authority on me to decide who got what. I would exercise that authority only after first trying to reach an accommodation with each company.

The confidential meetings at Treasury were often emotional and contentious. Anecdotal evidence about the top twenty-five corporate executives—their ongoing importance to the company and their lack of involvement in earlier decisions that had almost brought down the business—dominated the discussions. Competitive statistical comparisons were secondary and ineffective as argument; we at Treasury possessed the same data and knew how to interpret the numbers. But the human element—that was something else again.

It became very personal. I discovered that contrary to public perception, compensation meant much more to a senior corporate official than mere material gain. Although not minimizing the benefits of wealth—a second home at the beach, a second (or third) automobile in the driveway, private schools for the children—most corporate executives who came to see me emphasized that adequate compensation was a symbol of self-worth. Compensation mirrored individual fulfillment, that without generous pay, company officials would view themselves as failures. Individual success could be determined only by comparing oneself to the competition, and dollars paid would be the deciding factor. By comparison, family, friendship, and community respect paled in significance.

This narrow vision of what defines a life fueled occasional emotional outbursts by corporate executives: "Why are you demeaning my individual success? Why don't you acknowledge my value to the company? Why don't you believe in all that I have accomplished?" And they really believed these arguments, convinced that compensation was the only appropriate measure of success. To these business leaders, these captains of industry, these officials, the special master was evaluating their true worth—to the company, to society, to themselves.

I recalled the famous scene in Frank Loesser's Broadway musical *How to Succeed in Business Without Really Trying,* in which J. Pierrepont Finch, a clever young window cleaner with a hankering for corporate advancement, gives himself a personal pep talk in front of a mirror. He assures himself he is a paragon of wisdom, judgment, talent, and drive, each verse of comically inflated self-praise ending with the refrain "I believe in you!" Sometimes the pay hearings made me feel as if America's corporate suites were populated by platoons of insecure J. Pierrepont Finches, all desperate to have their worth validated—preferably by a paycheck containing as many zeroes as possible.

Trying to separate my work from its inherent emotional impact wasn't easy. To add an element of consistent, objective rationality to the process, I developed five principles that I followed throughout:

- Guaranteed cash salary would be limited to $500,000 per year; any additional amount would require special master approval. (In the end, fewer than 10 percent of the officials in the seven companies received such approval.)
- Cash bonuses were prohibited. Any remaining annual compensation would be in the form of company stock that, by law, would vest immediately and be valued on the day of issuance. But this stock could be redeemed only in three equal annual installments beginning in 2011 (with each installment redeemable one year earlier if TARP obligations were repaid). In this manner, individual compensation would be tied to company-wide performance over the long term.
- Additional bonus payments could be made, but only in the form of "long-term restricted stock," which required individual executives to remain employed at the company for at least three years after the stock was issued. Even then it could be redeemed only in 25 percent increments for each 25 percent of TARP repaid to the taxpayer.
- Any other individual compensation and perquisites, such as private plane travel and country club dues, would be limited to $25,000; any additional amount would require special master approval.

- Deferred compensation pursuant to retirement programs and severance arrangements were frozen at 2009 levels; special additional compensation for senior corporate officials exiting the company was prohibited.

In the end, General Motors and Chrysler, and their financing arms, GMAC and Chrysler Financial, did not prove to be much of a problem. Struggling to survive (GM had just completed its bankruptcy reorganization and Chrysler Financial was planning to close its doors), these four companies could not afford to present compensation packages that raised eyebrows. So fixing compensation for the auto industry and its financial partners was relatively simple and straightforward. Everybody (other than the CEO or CFO) received total all-in compensation packages well under $1 million per year, with few financial perks and little in the way of long-term stock. If my pay determinations for the auto industry were not exactly aligned with Main Street, they were unlikely to trigger an angry response from a public focused on Wall Street excesses.

The special master's 2009 and 2010 compensation determinations for the four auto industry companies were announced with little fanfare and even less commotion. The public and Congress did not seem to care. They had their eyes on a different prize—the financial services industry represented by AIG, Bank of America, and Citigroup—especially after my office released figures showing that the top *three* corporate officials at both Citigroup and Bank of America were requesting more annual compensation than the *combined* pay packages of all twenty-five individuals at GM or Chrysler.

The three financial giants each took a different tack when it came to dealing with the special master.

Citigroup was the easiest, primarily because all of our negotiations were with Lewis Kaden, a company lawyer and vice president with a healthy dose of political savvy and experience. I had known Kaden for twenty years and our relationship was grounded in mutual respect and admiration. Kaden realized that doing battle with the special master made little political or substantive sense; at the end of the day I would be making the ultimate compensation decisions. So, Kaden and Citigroup decided to pursue a sensible course of action based on the realities of the moment: offer sensible compensation proposals, negotiate the best deal possible, and ultimately accept the results as inevitable.

This strategy was immediately put to the test when it came to Andrew J. Hall and PHIBRO, a Citigroup subsidiary energy trading unit. Hall had a contract with Citigroup entitling him to receive more than $95 million in bonus compensation! This was far and away the biggest such package I had to handle. (A second executive was pegged to receive more than $30 million.) Meeting with Kaden in New York City, I warned him that there was no way I would approve such compensation: "I don't care if Hall has a binding contract written in stone. He can go to court to try and get it. He won't get $95 million on my watch. Talk about compensation based on taking 'excessive risk.' Anybody receiving a bonus of $95 million must be engaged in risky transactions. Hall is the poster child showing how pay promotes risk. Congress will schedule a ten-camera hearing with Hall being the featured witness. You better do something about this."

Within a few weeks, prior to the announcement of my Citigroup compensation determinations, the company sold PHIBRO to Occidental Petroleum for a bargain-basement price. Because Occidental had not received any TARP assistance and was not subject to my jurisdiction, it could negotiate a compensation package with Hall without government interference. A showdown was averted. To this day I have no idea what Occidental paid Hall in the end.

In all other cases involving Citigroup officials, Kaden and I negotiated acceptable compensation packages that were competitive in the industry. The total packages were high—most senior Citigroup officials received in excess of $2 million each—but the guaranteed base salary cash component for each individual was more modest, less than $500,000. The remaining pay took the form of long-term stock, which could not be redeemed for at least three years. And the CEO of Citigroup, Vikram Pandit, accepted no salary or bonus compensation. By back-channeling with Kaden and negotiating pay individual by individual, we reached agreement with the company.

Bank of America was different. Negotiations began in a spirit of cooperation. I convinced retiring CEO Kenneth D. Lewis that it was in his interest, as well as that of the bank, for him to return his entire 2009 compensation. I pointed out that in his thirty-year career at the bank, Lewis had amassed a retirement pension and severance package in excess of $50 million. "Be sensible," I told his lawyer. "What is one year's salary to Lewis? He is walking away with $50 million, guaranteed and airtight. Do you want him dragged before Congress to justify his salary as he departs?" Lewis agreed, and another battle was averted.

My discussions with Bank of America Vice President Steele Alphin were cordial enough. But we could not reach agreement on about a half dozen other senior bank officials. The reason could be traced to the bank's earlier purchase of Merrill Lynch and its top traders, each earning $10 million to $30 million a year. I reminded Alphin that Bank of America was, after all, a bank and that no top-twenty-five official would earn anything like double-digit millions on my watch. Alphin was incredulous. The Merrill Lynch traders had arrived at the bank with a track record of making upward of $10 million. He warned that if I didn't continue the pay scale, they would quickly leave for a competitor. Some modest reduction might be acceptable, but a sharp reduction in pay would send them to the exits. The bank could not afford to lose them.

I was unmoved. First I reminded Alphin that he was ignoring political realities. If I authorized the compensation he was requesting, we would both end up being attacked by Republicans and Democrats alike at a congressional hearing. The traders themselves would be called on the carpet to explain their pay. It would be a public relations disaster for both them and the bank. Second, what about the compensation culture at the bank itself, and the effect of such pay on loyal, longtime bank officials who were not previously employed by Merrill Lynch? I warned Alphin that his pay recommendations could drive a wedge between the two camps trying to coexist. He was being shortsighted in promoting such disparate pay; the bank itself would suffer in the long term from such compensation policies.

I advised him to heed my words. The special master was only trying to save the capitalists from themselves! A political tin ear would inevitably result in more Draconian government intervention.

But we could not agree. So I imposed compensation packages for the top twenty-five officials at the bank, including the former Merrill Lynch traders. Some would still receive up to $9 million but, again, only a small amount was guaranteed as cash salary, with the remainder in long-term bank stock.

Alphin retired within a matter of weeks.

The most emotional battle involved financial services giant AIG. It was not cordial or pretty. It was a heavyweight bout with the gloves off. In one corner stood Robert Benmosche, the new CEO of AIG, smart and combative, who decided to become an active front-line participant in the Treasury discussions.

The very embodiment of "too big to fail," AIG had been in the crosshairs of Congress from the beginning. It was the most visible symbol of all that was wrong with Wall Street. When AIG's former CEO, Ed Liddy, had testified earlier before the House Banking Committee that certain AIG employees in the financial products division would receive $165 million in guaranteed retention bonuses—even after receiving TARP subsidies from the taxpayers—Congress howled. It was the financial products division that had brought down AIG. How could these very employees be awarded $165 million in bonus compensation? Liddy had tried to explain that AIG was obligated to make these bonus payments under contracts that had been signed before the financial debacle. And he had legal opinions from lawyers at both AIG and the Federal Reserve confirming this obligation. But congressional leaders remained furious.

Now those old guaranteed contracts were up for negotiation between Liddy's successor and me.

Benmosche made it very personal, promoting morale within the beleaguered company by offering to brave public criticism while supporting AIG executives. He enlisted the support of some very credible seconds in the government—Treasury officials in the Office of Financial Stability and high-ranking deputies at the Federal Reserve in New York City. Benmosche laid down the gauntlet: meet AIG's compensation demands or risk company bankruptcy and the loss of the taxpayers' money.

Many government officials were ready to blink. But not Neal Wolin. "Ken, work it out with Benmosche," he said. "Don't cave, but don't push him over the edge. You know the breaking point. We need to protect the taxpayers' investment."

I met with Benmosche on about a half dozen occasions in the Treasury building. I liked him. Despite all of his bluster, I sized him up as a deal maker, a poker player who would never disclose when he was bluffing. He knew how to close a deal. And he had a personal, vested interest in working out pay issues involving his senior AIG employees. Failure was not an option while he was in charge.

But it would not be easy.

Over months of discussions with Benmosche and others at AIG, I confronted foursquare those guaranteed retention contracts, some going as far back as 2005. Benmosche (and others at Treasury) demanded that they be honored. They did the simple math—after calculating appropriate pay for each AIG official, add to the bottom line any retention bonuses due.

I balked. Some of these individual bonuses exceeded $1 million. Three key senior executives in the financial products division, whose compensation ranged from $1.5 million to $2.4 million, were demanding overdue huge retention bonus payments. Awarding these officials their bonuses in a post-TARP world would ignite a political firestorm in Congress, and it could not be justified on the merits. Changed circumstances—the global financial crisis and threatened AIG demise—surely altered the original expectations of the contracting parties. The retention contracts were unenforceable in post-2008 America. The world had changed—along with the fortunes of AIG.

At the same time, though I did not let on to Benmosche, I agreed with everybody at Treasury that it would be a huge public policy mistake to mount a court challenge to the validity of these retention contracts. Sanctity of contract, enshrined in our Constitution, could not be lightly disregarded, especially by the Department of the Treasury and the Federal Reserve, steadfast pillars of our financial system. Asking creative lawyers to find loopholes in existing contracts entered into by private parties in good faith was not a viable option.

But the world *had* changed since the signing of these bonus contracts. Surely, I argued, changed circumstances compelled voluntary reformation of the contracts.

Now it was Benmosche's turn to push back. First he joined the common chorus, warning that if the old contracts were not honored, key AIG employees in the financial products division, who had nothing to do with the earlier financial crisis, would leave, threatening AIG's financial future and the taxpayers' investment. "Ken," Benmosche pleaded, "I am trying to rebuild this company. You are not making it easy. The dollars in dispute are nothing compared to what is at stake."

I offered a solution. In line with one of my five compensation principles, I urged Benmosche to take the retention bonus money and convert it into long-term AIG stock. Instead of giving AIG employees immediate cash, they would invest it in the company's future. If AIG succeeded, their stock would increase in value and they would be handsomely rewarded; if it tanked, they would lose their investment. Consistent with our regulations, their financial future would be tied to the company they served. This solution had already been accepted by some individuals owed retention bonuses at both Bank of America and Citigroup. Why not do the same at AIG?

To my surprise this proposal was also rejected, not only by Benmosche but also by Treasury and the Federal Reserve. They all contended that AIG's financial future was so perilous and uncertain that trading cash for stock could not be justified. Bank of America and Citigroup were in a different financial posture— though they had needed the government's help, their future was optimistic. AIG was flat on its back, its stock virtually worthless. When I reminded my critics at AIG, Treasury, and the Federal Reserve that the stock was currently selling at more than $30 a share, they responded that it was all speculative. In reality, it was not worth even $3 a share!

I was shocked to hear this. The implication was that it was okay for the public to invest in AIG's future, even as AIG's own senior employees were unwilling to make a similar commitment to their own company.

I offered an alternative. Treasury regulations permitted the special master to factor past due bonus money into calculations determining present pay. Money was fungible. If a senior AIG official was entitled to a pre-TARP retention bonus, we could consider this in calculating the official's bottom-line net pay, past *and* present.

Benmosche agreed, and we began the arduous task of negotiating individual pay packages for each AIG official, with retention bonus money thrown into the mix: How much cash? How much stock? How much of a discount in bottom-line dollars to account for past bonus compensation now overdue? What level of compensation would keep AIG personnel at their desks? How much would they be willing to discount their cash to avoid public and political criticism? Somehow I had to satisfy all my constituents—Benmosche, senior AIG executives, officials at both Treasury and the Federal Reserve, and my colleagues in the special master's office. It took months to hammer out the individual compensation packages.

But I demanded one more concession from Benmosche. After Liddy had testified in Congress, certain AIG officials who had already received retention bonus payments had publicly promised to return this money, totaling $45 million, to the taxpayers. They had not done so, and the public was watching. I conditioned our new deal on Benmosche's making it happen. He agreed. And as promised, individual AIG officials paid in full the $45 million before the prospective pay packages were announced.

There was one more issue I had to wrestle with: lateral hires. This was exemplified at the highest level by Bank of America's search for a new CEO in the wake of Kenneth Lewis's retirement.

Under the rules of the game, the special master would have to approve any proposed compensation package. And any credible, experienced lateral hire (that is, someone already serving as a CEO at a comparable company) would come to the bank with an existing compensation package that would never pass muster—millions in guaranteed cash, a vested pension plan in the double-digit millions, a severance package of additional millions, and a demand for such financial perks as a private jet for personal use and the payment of country club dues. On two occasions the bank sought my guidance and ultimate approval to hire a new CEO from a competing bank. Each time I rejected the proposed pay arrangements, reminding the bank that it was ignoring political realities.

"Why not promote somebody already employed at the bank?" I finally suggested. It was the only logical way to avoid the lateral-hire dilemma. Bank of America finally agreed. It had no choice. It would elevate one of its own as Lewis's successor.

On October 22, 2009, the Office of the Special Master publicly announced the compensation determinations for the top twenty-five corporate officials in each of the seven companies. Applying my five principles had a major financial effect on senior company executives. Individual cash compensation was reduced by approximately 90 percent from 2008 levels, and overall compensation dropped by 50 percent from 2008. Only three corporate executives received base cash salaries greater than $1 million: Benmosche and two senior officials at Chrysler Financial (which was planning to go out of business and could not award any long-term incentives other than cash).

Unlike past pay practices, which allowed executives to sell their stock immediately, the special master's rulings required that stock be held for the long term and that corporate executive compensation be inextricably linked to company performance. My rulings also prohibited any special retirement or severance compensation beyond that available to the company's everyday workers.

In the press conference announcing my determinations, I took the offensive, highlighting the cuts we had made, the reductions in guaranteed cash, the need for the companies to thrive if corporate officials were to be paid additional compensation, and an end to exorbitant perks. I reminded all who would listen that my jurisdiction was, after all, limited to just 175 corporate officials—hardly an assault on the entire free enterprise system. During the next week I appeared frequently on television and radio, extolling the virtues of my rulings and expressing the hope that they could act as a model that other companies could adopt voluntarily. And I braced for the wave of criticism from both sides that I had always expected.

The seven companies themselves were not pleased. They complained privately to anybody and everybody in the Treasury building that my compensation determinations threatened to relegate the companies to secondary status, unable to attract necessary talent.

Publicly, however, six of the seven companies expressed satisfaction with the results. They issued public statements taking the high road, declaring that the compensation determinations would not inhibit their ability to compete and that they would abide by the decisions and work to restore the companies to financial health.

But not Bank of America. Stating that my compensation determinations were too onerous, unfair, and counterproductive, bank officials offered dire warnings about future competitiveness and the bank's ability to flourish. The special master had blithely ignored the practical realities confronting the bank and its competitors. The bank would not put on a smiling face merely to please the public.

Meanwhile, public reaction to my compensation determinations was surprisingly positive. I'd expected attacks criticizing my unwillingness to demand even greater cuts in corporate pay. None came. Officials at the Treasury Department—and, I assume, at the White House—exhaled. Wolin's plan had succeeded with muted public fuss and bother.

In the end—perhaps ironically—the interests of Treasury, the Office of the Special Master, and the seven companies were all aligned. Eager to escape future scrutiny by the special master, three of the companies did what was necessary to free themselves from my oversight. Bank of America actually *borrowed* the funds needed to pay back the taxpayer in full, thereby escaping my jurisdiction. (Shares in Bank of America rose 3 percent following the repayment announcement.) Citigroup followed in a matter of months; so did Chrysler Financial.

It took this roundabout final act to ensure that the new law's ultimate objective be fulfilled at last: the taxpayers had been made whole. And three of the seven companies could once again go their own way when it came to pay, rejoining the traditional free enterprise system we've always cherished.

Nor, despite the dark warnings, was there any mass exodus of executive talent from these companies. To the contrary, 85 percent of the individuals whose pay was determined by the special master remained at their desks during the following year. This made a great deal of practical sense. It is not so easy for a senior member of corporate management, long identified with a company brand and familiar with a well-defined corporate culture, simply to move across the street (or across the ocean) and join a competitor. How marketable is such an individual? How risk averse is he or she after so many years at a company? There is a certain comfort level in remaining in place, well paid, respected, and generally satisfied with the business environment. Your colleagues are not only business associates but friends of long standing; you eat, work, and socialize together; the commute from home to work is familiar and comfortable. Familiarity breeds confidence. And as for the 15 percent who left the company following my pay decisions, it is not at all clear that their departure was tied to compensation. Corporate officials leave for myriad reasons, including retirement. Pay was only one possible factor.

I confronted one final challenge: the law and regulations had conferred on the special master wide-ranging discretion to "clawback," or seek to recover compensation previously provided to corporate officials at *any* company that had received TARP financial assistance. There were over 450 such companies. In conferring this power to the special master, Congress was expressing its belief that the corporate titans responsible for the financial crisis should not be able to escape intact. The special master therefore had the authority—if he decided to exercise it—to attempt to recoup whatever he determined to be appropriate. He could seek to recover billions—or nothing at all.

For months I wavered on the issue. It made some political sense to mount an offensive against those perceived to be responsible for America's financial peril. It would be political theater of a high order. Besides, some companies had infamously used TARP money to pay bonuses to high-level executives. The public would cheer any effort to recover these funds.

But I hesitated. I knew that seeking to recover such compensation would be almost impossible. Lawsuits would be necessary.

Few, if any, officials would voluntarily return their own money to the Treasury. And the lawsuits might very well prove costly and unsuccessful. These individuals had violated no law or regulation; creative lawyering might be effective, but at what price and over what period of time? Finally, I was troubled by the idea that I would become an armchair quarterback second-guessing previous pay decisions.

Neal Wolin shared my concern: "Be careful. Treasury should not be in the business of trying to recover pay from individuals who were entitled to the money at the time. Besides, we want these companies back on their feet, not fighting us in the courtroom."

I decided not to exercise *any* of my "clawback" authority. Instead the special master promulgated a new regulation, purely prospective, urging all companies that received any TARP assistance to adopt a new "brake provision." If a company found itself in financial peril (as designated by government regulators), it would no longer be required to honor previous individual compensation contracts. Instead, "brakes" would be placed on otherwise legally binding compensation obligations; contracts could be voided based upon unanticipated financial consequences.

The rule was purely voluntary. No company was compelled to adopt it. Once again I was seeking a form of compensation compromise that would offer the Congress some political and substantive satisfaction that it was no longer "business as usual" on Wall Street. Without a proposed "brake provision," or some similar measure offered as a substitute for exercising my "clawback" authority, I anticipated adverse political fallout—and perhaps something worse in the form of new legislation targeting Wall Street.

I knew that no company would agree to the "brake provision"—at least voluntarily. The idea not only would promote contractual uncertainty, but it also would place companies at a distinct competitive disadvantage. Corporations would have difficulty attracting the talent they needed if potential candidates knew their "ironclad" compensation contracts were not binding but could be declared null and void—and by the government, no less.

To this day, I know of no company that has ratified the special master's brake provision. But I still believe it would be a good idea for American business in the long run. Just don't expect Congress, any federal regulatory agency, or corporate America to agree with me.

It's too early to tell whether, and to what extent, the special master's pay decisions will have any lasting value. But I am dubious.

For one thing, interest has waned. By the middle of 2011, the new focus of populist discontent was on the Occupy Movement, a series of public demonstrations in cities around the world demanding broad changes in how corporations are structured, do business, influence public policy, and get paid. Despite the Occupy Movement's interest in income inequality, the attention of Congress, the public, and the media has decisively moved on from the special master's office at Treasury—now ably filled by my replacement, Patricia Geoghegan, who continues to determine pay packages for the four companies still subject to her jurisdiction: AIG, Chrysler, GM, and GM's new financing arm, Ally.

This should surprise no one. Historically, laissez-faire capitalism and private free market forces have determined pay. Neither

Congress nor the executive branch disagrees. Both branches of government made it clear to me that I was engaged in political showmanship, implementing a policy more symbolic than real, the focus restricted to just seven companies and 175 individuals. The real work of financial and economic reform would be done elsewhere: Dodd/Frank legislation, the federal regulatory agencies, and the G-20. Corporate governance reform providing shareholders with new authority over pay is now required by statute (Dodd/Frank). Meanwhile, the SEC is promoting the idea of transparency, that internal corporate decision-making involving compensation be subject to sunlight and open debate. And the Federal Reserve and FDIC have promulgated new compensation principles that track much of what we required at Treasury. Finally, Secretary Geithner himself has taken the lead in urging G-20 foreign leaders to impose similar regulatory pay rules so that American companies are not placed at a competitive disadvantage.

One conclusion is clear: nobody should expect corporate America to voluntarily accept my compensation determinations as a guide to their future pay policies. Why should they? In past times of public anger over financial industry excesses, Wall Street has played a waiting game, lying low until the political storm subsides. History is on Wall Street's side, at least when it comes to government fine-tuning of corporate internal decision-making. Add to this the government deregulation philosophy that followed in the wake of the Reagan administration, and it is easy to see why American businesses are emboldened when it comes to pay. To most on Wall Street, the seven companies had only themselves to blame for Treasury's interference. They assumed that such interference would never, ever apply to them. And they're almost certainly right.

Like many of my other public-interest assignments, the congressional decision to regulate corporate pay was an aberration. The government is not in the habit of fixing private pay, nor should it be. The circumstances of the TARP bailout, the financial system collapse, and the public anger aimed at Wall Street triggered a unique political response.

Did the limits we imposed on compensation for 175 corporate executives work as intended? That depends upon the objectives against which we measure the program.

Did it save the taxpayers money, as good-government advocates would demand? No. The compensation limits didn't reduce the TARP moneys already provided to the seven companies. But if smaller compensation packages to corporate executives helped improve the companies' profit margins, then the limitations and restrictions played at least a modest role in bolstering the financial system, as intended by the lawmakers who passed TARP in the first place.

Did the program have any lasting impact on Wall Street's compensation incentive structure, reducing the likelihood that executives would incur excessive risks in pursuit of huge personal gain? Probably not. Financial services firms, in particular, have not dramatically reformed their bonus systems. Market forces and diminished profits have had some impact leading to reduced Wall Street pay, but I doubt these reductions are attributable to the special master's work.

As I mentioned, the proposed "brake provision" to be inserted into employee contracts has not been adopted by any financial services firm. It seems that an even more catastrophic collapse may be necessary before corporate executives decide to voluntarily limit their risk-taking in pursuit of profits.

But did the program defuse the political issue of populist anger directed at excessive earnings by "fat cat" bankers? Apparently it did—at least to the extent that neither the program itself nor the compensation packages directed at the 175 top bailed-out executives ever attracted the controversy and hostility I initially expected.

As symbolic gestures go, the statute was effective—and this, of course, is exactly what Congress intended.

– 6 –

OIL SPILL IN THE GULF OF MEXICO

"The Perfect Storm"

In my first several missions to determine who gets what—for the victims of Agent Orange, the 9/11 terrorist attacks, and the Virginia Tech shootings—the American people were on my side, an important ingredient in any recipe for success. It might take months, or even years, for the victims themselves to grudgingly acknowledge my compensation efforts as fair and reasonable. But the average Joe, the everyday American, was in my corner. Even when serving as the Treasury's "pay czar," I was David attempting to rein in the Goliaths of Wall Street, and so benefited from public support. This provided me with a certain degree of political immunity from the criticism of elected officials and those with a personal interest in the outcomes.

But what might happen when citizen acclaim did not come with the job? What if a unique American tragedy gave rise to a parade of horribles that would challenge my ability to determine who got what?

What if the patriotism and public compassion that character-ized the Agent Orange, 9/11, and Virginia Tech payment programs were absent?

What if the underlying tragedy could be traced not to foreign enemies, a deranged gunman, or even the vagaries of a poorly reg-ulated financial marketplace, but rather to an acknowledged cor-porate wrongdoer, still alive and reaping billions in profits?

What if that tragedy dominated media attention for months, permitting the American people to witness the unfolding events firsthand, on a daily basis, stoking public outrage and igniting calls for punishment?

What if elected officials—federal, state, and local—saw the tragedy as an opportunity to score political points, reaffirming their commitment and allegiance to the voters they represented through demands for compensation?

What if the overwhelming majority of the damage claims aris-ing from the tragedy involved not death or physical injury, but rather claims for lost jobs and wages, reduced business income, and other hard-to-measure, hard-to-prove costs?

What if the lawyers—whose cooperation was instrumental in ensuring the success of the previous compensation programs—now opposed any fast-track compensation alternative to the traditional litigation system?

What if the administrator chosen to design and implement such a compensation program were to inherit a payment system already established by the corporate wrongdoer itself?

What if the administrator decided to be compensated for designing and administering the new payment program rather than do the job pro bono? And what if that compensation were to come from the very corporation that acknowledged responsibility for the tragedy?

And finally, what if the volume and complexity of claims dwarfed anything previously experienced, making promises by both the federal government and the guilty corporation that the many, many victims would be "made whole" exceedingly difficult, if not impossible, to keep?

Fashioning a new payment program that would overcome not one or two but *all* of these variables would pose an unprecedented challenge to any administrator. In determining who gets what, the administrator confronts a "perfect storm" that threatens the very life of the program. Navigating it would require competence, creativity, confidence, patience and, above all, a readiness to engage the critics forthrightly and boldly.

It all began in the Gulf of Mexico.

On April 20, 2010, the Deepwater Horizon oil rig, owned by Transocean and operated by BP, exploded, killing eleven rig workers, injuring hundreds, and spewing millions of gallons of natural raw oil into the Gulf. As the world watched live television footage, oil gushed from the damaged well almost 5,000 feet below the surface. The damage was so profound, the leak located so deep, that neither BP nor the US Coast Guard was immediately able to cap the well and stem the flow of oil. For more than twelve weeks, oil continued to rush to the surface while corporate and public officials weighed desperate measures to contain the disaster.

The complex technology that permitted deepwater drilling in the Gulf, miles below the surface, had outpaced the ability of government and industry to confront and overcome an unprecedented environmental nightmare. Following Gulf currents, a vast thick black oil slick, miles wide, threatened Gulf waters and beaches stretching from Pensacola, Florida, to Alabama's Mobile Bay; from Mississippi's shoreline near Biloxi to Louisiana's fishing grounds; all the way to the Texas shore near Galveston.

The story was splashed across front pages around the globe. Daily media accounts highlighted the magnitude and scope of the disaster, throwing punch after punch at the perceived ineptitude of BP and the Coast Guard. For Americans, BP became public enemy number one, a foreign corporation that had placed oil profits ahead of safety. Together with its corporate partners—Transocean, Halliburton, Anadarko, and others—BP was tried and convicted in the court of public opinion. Meanwhile, cable news commentators declared that the disaster was worse than Hurricane Katrina; the oil rig explosion was no act of God but the result of corporate recklessness in the unending search for profit. The public was horrified and fascinated—and cable network ratings soared.

The companies commenced finger-pointing without delay. BP blamed Transocean, the owner of the oil rig; both in turn pointed to Halliburton, the rig cement contractor. Other companies with ties to the construction and operation of the rig were accused of negligence. Meanwhile, allegations of the government's incompetence in failing to contain the oil slick triggered memories of Katrina's aftermath and the woeful performance of federal, state, and local governments in responding to the plight of New Orleans's residents after the hurricane.

The public demanded action—and an accounting.

The young Obama administration was determined to take the offensive. Even while the oil continued to gush from the damaged well, the president himself summoned senior BP officials to the White House for a woodshed lecture. Exiting from the meeting, representatives of BP acknowledged the company's responsibility for the catastrophe. Not only that, at the president's urging—some would later call it arm-twisting—BP publicly agreed to create a compensation fund of $20 billion to pay all victims, individuals and businesses, harmed by the spill (though without admitting any legal liability).

Nothing like this had ever occurred in American history. There was no new statute, no congressional hearings, no official administrative regulations, no court order—just a private agreement orchestrated by the president to be implemented by BP and monitored by the Department of Justice. An escrow agreement signed by BP and the department would formalize the commitment. One of the world's giant oil companies simply agreed to enter the claims compensation business.

How did this happen? BP easily could have used the courts as a safe haven, litigating for decades, denying any legal responsibility, and paying millions to the lawyers but not one cent to claimants. The Exxon *Valdez* oil disaster in Alaska was litigated for twenty years according to this exact strategy.

Yet BP had its reasons for this decision. For one thing, BP executives realized they were confronted with a public relations disaster of unparalleled magnitude and serious practical implications.

BP's vast drilling operations in the Gulf of Mexico required federal regulatory approval. Locking horns with the federal government would be a costly strategy—particularly at a time when voters were furious and eager for a scapegoat.

Second, presidential spin notwithstanding, the deal was hardly one-sided. Decades of litigation with no end in sight would have led to corporate financial uncertainty magnified by the unpredictability of the American legal system. Following the oil rig explosion, the value of BP stock plunged dramatically. As the company's leadership was well aware, media financial experts were focusing their attention on the possibility of bankruptcy. Would-be investors paused before committing to new oil drilling projects. A strategy of litigation modeled after the example of the Exxon *Valdez* carried with it stark consequences.

Instead BP opted for an alternative approach. The well-publicized $20 billion handshake would create a unique private administrative claims process, offering all potential litigants the choice of avoiding a protracted legal nightmare and securing compensation quickly.

By announcing a $20 billion pledge, BP was also agreeing to defer any final accounting with other potential defendant contributors, such as Transocean and Halliburton, which were not part of the escrow agreement. That would come later, either inside or outside of the courtroom. For now BP set its sights on the immediate goal: to anticipate and contain litigation. Paying the victims of the Gulf oil spill would be the top priority.

BP's executives had also weighed the impact of the Federal Oil Pollution Act (OPA), enacted into law after Exxon *Valdez*. This complex statute anticipated that following an oil spill, the oil company responsible would step up and honor all eligible claims for compensation. Allocating responsibility among joint defendants would come later. OPA was the law of the land, and BP was certainly mindful of its legal obligations under the statute.

For all of these reasons, BP's decision was an informed one based on its own best business interests—far from the presidential "shakedown" denounced by Texas Congressman Joseph Barton (although President Obama might wear Barton's comment as a badge of honor).

But compensating the victims of the oil spill posed challenges that no corporation had ever confronted.

In addition to the sheer volume of potential claimants—millions of individuals and businesses residing and doing business in the Gulf region—the nature and quality of the claims would have to be evaluated one by one. Unlike those of Agent Orange, 9/11, and Virginia Tech, Gulf compensation claims would involve individual damage calculations pertaining to lost wages and income, the inability to work or run a business because of the oil spill. Economic damages, not loss of life and limb, would be the center of attention. The total universe of claims would include only a modest number of individuals asserting death of a loved one or physical injury caused by the rig explosion and subsequent oil spill.

In addition, there was the problem of proof. It would not be enough for a claimant simply to allege damage; individuals and businesses would need to offer at least some evidence—tax returns, corporate business records and profit and loss statements, checkbooks, pay stubs—verifying their loss. Mere assertions would not be sufficient—payment of a claim could be justified only by proof. But how to define the nature of that proof, and

how much to require? Pay formulas could be written and calculation methodologies announced, but consideration of each and every
claim would be required.

BP was in no position to do this. It had neither the expertise
nor the desire to micromanage a proposed claims process. Besides,
the "handshake" with the president required that BP distance itself from evaluating individual claims. The escrow agreement instead contemplated an independent claims process, with neither
BP nor the administration reviewing each and every claim—a wise
decision. If the government had been in charge of such a claims
program, there would have been an enormous amount of political
risk associated with every decision.

The only solution was to create a new and independent body to
make whole the victims of the oil spill. It was to be a unique hybrid
claims process—standing in the shoes of BP pursuant to the company's OPA-mandated responsibilities, while at the same time dis-
tancing itself from both BP and the administration when it came to
evaluating individual claims. This dual approach was something
new—policy makers had never attempted anything like it. But the
magnitude of the environmental disaster in the Gulf and, just as
important, the politics of disaster relief post-Katrina compelled the
administration and BP to try this new system. In theory at least,
everybody would benefit: eligible claimants would be paid quickly
without waiting for the anticipated litigation to run its course; BP
would avoid the specter of the Exxon *Valdez* lawsuit nightmare;
and a new administration would receive high marks for orchestrating the creation of a $20 billion private fund (requiring no tax-
payer money) to compensate victims.

But achieving these goals would not be easy. The escrow agreement contemplated the selection of a claims administrator who would have the substantive and political expertise to get the job done. This administrator would also need the mental and emotional toughness required to withstand the criticism and abuse that would inevitably arise in the course of paying—and denying—hundreds of thousands of individual claims.

I was in Washington in May 2010, a month after the spill, when I received a call from Tom Milch, chairman of the distinguished Washington law firm of Arnold & Porter. Milch is a blue-chip environmental lawyer, well known and respected throughout the nation, with whom I'd worked closely a few years earlier in connection with his firm's representation of 9/11 victims. I'd been impressed not only with his legal competence and mastery of detail but also with his thoughtful demeanor and sound judgment. He did not rattle easily; he thrived on solving tough legal problems and was a creative thinker always looking for imaginative solutions while remaining calm and cool under pressure. It was no accident that he was now managing one of the nation's premier law firms.

"Ken, I've been retained by BP in connection with this Deepwater disaster. As you know, the company has agreed to put up $20 billion to pay claims and other costs in the Gulf. But it needs somebody to do it. I've suggested you, and BP officials in Houston are interested. They are already paying claims, but they need a credible independent administrator and claims program to take charge. Are you interested?"

I expressed a keen interest but suggested that my 9/11 experience would be of limited value in dealing with these claims: "There will be thousands of claims involving business damage, not death. You need accountants, not lawyers. But if BP wants me, I am more than interested. Just make sure the administration is on board."

Milch's response was typical: "Stand by. I need to work this at my end."

A few weeks went by. I heard nothing. Then a second call, followed by a meeting with just the two of us at Milch's law firm: "BP is interested. They need references. Also, remember, the administration must approve."

This was the easy part. I offered up references: Judge Jack Weinstein, Attorney General John Ashcroft, President Charles Steger of Virginia Tech, and Neal Wolin at Treasury. The next step would be a visit to Houston to meet with BP officials. Milch's plan reflected his personality: calm, deliberate, step-by-step, confident. He clearly knew the endgame and how to get there.

In two Houston meetings, and another series of meetings in Washington, I met with the leaders of BP, while others participated by live video conferencing from BP headquarters in London: the new CEO, Robert Dudley; general counsel Rupert Bondy; the head of BP North America, Lamar McKay; Geir Robinson, vice president of exploration and production; and key in-house lawyers Jack Lynch and Mark Holstein. The chairman of the BP board, Carl-Henric Svanberg, also paid a visit to my Washington office, sizing me up and learning firsthand of my plans for designing and administering a claims program. He would be reporting back to his full board in London. Milch was directing traffic and orchestrating the plan, but BP was cautious, incisive, and deliberate.

They had many questions. Why Feinberg? How independent will he be? How beholden to the administration and the plaintiff lawyers? What input will BP have in creating the claims program and reviewing individual claims? Who will Feinberg retain to help him? What will the claims infrastructure look like? What will it cost? How long will it take? These inquiries—always friendly, never combative, clearly focused—triggered hours of discussion over the ensuing weeks.

I offered preliminary suggestions about what the claims program might look like. Milch warned me: "Ken, don't push, don't promote, don't argue. Educating BP is the goal. They need to become comfortable with the entire idea."

He was right. It took a month for BP officials to warm to me and my ideas for a claims program. Milch kept me informed as they called my references, deliberated among themselves, and considered other alternatives. At last, in June, they agreed to retain me as administrator of the new Gulf Coast Claims Facility (GCCF). Milch's master plan had succeeded—but only one party to the escrow agreement had yet agreed. The administration's approval was also required.

But if the BP selection process was slow and deliberative, Obama administration approval was quick and definitive. Who better than Feinberg, Senator Ted Kennedy's former chief of staff who had just recently taken the heat for Treasury as the Wall Street pay czar? I had the experience. If I was willing to lurch from one crisis to another and to battle a political firestorm in dealing with angry Gulf citizens clamoring for their share of $20 billion, it was fine with the administration. I had just one meeting with Associate Attorney General Tom Perrelli and his counsel Brian Hauck, the two point men for the administration. They quickly signed on, exhibiting the same characteristics as Milch: friendly, calm, confident, and, frankly, relieved that I was acceptable to BP. As Perrelli put it, "You won't hear much from us. It is your program to design and administer. We will distance ourselves from your day-to-day work. We will monitor, but not interfere. Good luck."

The message was clear: I could not expect any help from the Department of Justice or the White House in confronting the political fallout from the oil spill. That's exactly how it worked out. Only after I successfully completed my work—almost two years later—did I receive praise from the White House. The administration would justifiably take full credit for securing BP's $20 billion commitment to pay claims and other costs. But that is all the political credit it would seek. The rest was up to me.

Fortunately, in designing and administering the new GCCF, I benefited from a secret weapon: Deputy Administrator Camille Biros. I had first hired Biros as an administrative assistant in Senator Kennedy's office in 1978, but it quickly became apparent to everybody that her managerial and organizational skills far surpassed her technical competence. Smart, resolute, and dogged in her determination to do the job right, working sixteen-hour days, Biros had been at my side during all of my previous special assignments. Never one to suffer fools gladly, Biros demanded both quality performance and a work ethic rivaling her own. She set the bar very high but led the way in achieving it. One could agree or disagree with her decisions, but nobody could question her commitment, dedication, and loyalty. She was my first deputy, organizing and administering the GCCF claims process on a daily basis. And as the new claims program evolved, Biros assumed more and more responsibility, working with the lawyers and accountants in reviewing claims, proposing compensation methodologies, and interfacing with both BP and the Department of Justice. Everybody knew that when Biros spoke, she spoke for me.

Three others would complete the supervisory quartet at the top of the GCCF.

My law partner, Michael Rozen, had worked with me from the very first day he graduated Georgetown University Law Center (where he had been one of my very best students). One of the nation's best negotiators and mediators, his skills and strategic eye would prove essential in dealing with the determined, savvy plaintiff lawyers representing Gulf region claimants. Michael knew how to close, how to secure settlements; he would meet with lawyers ready to settle their claims.

Jacqueline Zins, a brilliant lawyer who had opted to work part-time while raising her family, became GCCF general counsel in all but name. Like Biros, Zins had a long history working with me, including the September 11th Victim Compensation Fund. When it came to legal issues, strategic decisions, and coordinating with outside lawyers, I trusted her judgment. And along with Biros, she exuded confidence and never hesitated to tell me what she thought, occasionally explaining why some of my ideas were unsound, impractical, or counterproductive. Loyalty built over decades permitted Zins to speak her mind. I welcomed her candor, always cloaked in friendship and mutual respect.

Charles "Chuck" Hacker would also prove to be a key player. A partner at PricewaterhouseCoopers, he was in charge of the PWC accounting team the GCCF retained to oversee the process for calculating damages. PWC had done an extraordinary job in providing accounting and claims services during my administration of the 9/11 fund, so a repeat performance was in order. Quiet and unassuming, Hacker had not been part of the earlier 9/11 effort. But his skill as an accountant was rivaled only by his strategic thinking about the overall claims process. Working with Biros, he would help administer the entire GCCF claims infrastructure in both Washington and the Gulf.

Two other entities would be critical to the successful creation of the GCCF. BrownGreer, headquartered in Richmond, Virginia, would help Biros design and implement the electronic claims review systems to be used in evaluating submissions and calculating damages. The Garden City Group of Lake Success, New York—a nationally respected claims processing firm—would be responsible for the intake and receipt of all claims and accompanying documentation. It would develop a master electronic database and cut checks to eligible claimants with documented damage.

The GCCF was scheduled to open its doors on August 23, 2010, so we had about sixty days to design claims procedures and create a claims infrastructure that would be ready to handle thousands of claims on day one. This itself would be a towering challenge. But we immediately confronted a complication that was unique in our experience.

Unlike our previous efforts, when we had designed a claims process with no existing program in place, here we were inheriting a preexisting BP claims initiative. BP had established thirty-five local claims offices throughout the Gulf region, some as far away as Key West and Key Largo in Florida, hundreds of miles from the oil spill. It had retained the services of Worley Catastrophe Response, a respected Louisiana insurance adjuster firm. More than 1,300 individual adjusters were in place throughout the Gulf and viewed themselves as pivotal to the overall success of the claims program, the front line of defense in dealing with disgruntled Gulf residents and businesses. Scrambling to demonstrate good faith and attempting to head off intense political criticism, Worley had authorized payment of almost $400 million to some 80,000 claimants. Yet in the four months since the oil spill, money had been doled out in a less-than-systematic manner. There was little consistency to the adjusters' process.

When I and my team came on the scene, we were confronted with a potential disaster. Each local office was an independent operation with minimal centralized administration. Claims adjusters were cutting checks on the spot to claimants demanding immediate payment. Proof of loss was determined then and there, as was evidence of damage linked to the spill. Claimants often visited multiple offices; if they were declared ineligible in one office, or the calculated damages were believed to be insufficient, a trip to a second office might lead to a different, more generous result.

As soon as we saw the results, we knew immediate changes would have to be made.

We replaced BP's balkanized system with centralized administration and controls. The thirty-five local offices would continue to function as claims intake centers, but their discretion to determine eligibility, calculate damages, and issue checks would end on August 23. Worley would remain in place working with the GCCF to help people submit their claims, but claimants could also file electronically on the GCCF website, or by fax or mail. To streamline the process and ensure consistency and fairness, all claims would be entered into a centralized database to be reviewed for completeness and eligibility based upon standardized criteria developed by the senior team at Feinberg Rozen in Washington. PWC accountants were responsible for the review and calculation of all business claims (which were more complex and problematic than relatively simple individual submissions). They would also review particularly complex claims that raised issues of precedential value. How far from the oil spill was the alleged damage? And what assumptions would govern in assessing the damage claims of new, start-up businesses? Checks would be cut by Citibank, which made arrangements with Whitney and Hancock Bank branches throughout the Gulf region to assist individual claimants with check cashing privileges.

But I underestimated the problems associated with inheriting an existing BP claims program. Managing claimant expectations posed a huge dilemma. Victims of the spill expected—in fact, demanded—that the new program be even more generous than the one it replaced. Wasn't the GCCF supposed to be independent from BP in making claimants whole? And it had $20 billion to dole out! Surely the new program would pick up where BP had left off and declare virtually everybody eligible. Gulf residents prepared for a steady stream of cash, assuming that demands for documentation would be minimal.

Biros and I assumed that keeping Worley personnel in place in the thirty-five claims offices would promote a seamless transition. We were wrong. By restricting Worley's local discretion and prohibiting Worley employees from making on-site determinations of eligibility, calculating damages, and cutting checks, we created a fertile environment for dissatisfaction and frustration. Claimants visiting local offices could no longer leave with a check in hand. Nor could they receive immediate, definitive information about their eligibility or damages. Worley personnel themselves expressed their own frustration in adjusting to the new GCCF system and my management team. They complained to anybody who would listen.

I would eventually retain the services of additional professionals throughout the Gulf region—lawyers from respected local law firms and credible claims processors from Louisiana and Mississippi—with no previous ties to Worley or the earlier BP claims operation. They would help me address citizen unhappiness. But the damage was already done. It would take months to dissipate claimant ill will.

In retrospect, the GCCF should have made a definitive break with the previous BP claims program. Instead, we encouraged both claimant and employee dissatisfaction and frustration. And unfortunately, this occurred at the very start of the process, when vulnerable and concerned citizens first visited a claims office seeking information.

This problem of inflated citizen expectation would gradually be handled in the only way possible—by delivering generous compensation to thousands of eligible claimants: $2.4 billion paid to 170,000 individuals and business in the first three months of the program. I learned over the years that any definition of success for a compensation program begins and ends with money freely flowing to those who qualify. Everything else is just talk. Although the GCCF would continue to be pummeled by its critics, the program's generosity would stand front and center as my first line of defense.

Compounding the problem of citizen expectations were questions surrounding my own personal compensation as GCCF administrator. How could I be truly independent of BP if the company was paying my salary? Didn't this pose a conflict of interest?

For the first time in my career I had to confront this issue of personal compensation. In my past service, in administering the September 11th Victim Compensation Fund, the Virginia Tech Hokie Spirit Memorial Fund, and the TARP Executive Compensation Program, I'd been able to deflect any criticism by claimants and corporate officials by citing the fact that I was not being compensated. Working pro bono immunized me from the charge that I had a vested interested in the outcome.

The BP oil spill was different. Here, I confronted an acknowledged wrongdoer, an international oil company prepared to admit some degree of culpability and front billions to compensate victims. My role as administrator would occupy my full attention for months or even years. I would be working out of a suitcase, constantly traveling to the Gulf to meet emotional victims of the oil spill. And as the point man, the visible face of the GCCF, I would bear the brunt of their criticism. Under the circumstances, I concluded that personal compensation was appropriate and justifiable. I simply would not work for nothing.

And who else but BP could possibly fund the entire initiative? You could not expect innocent claimants to pay a price of admission to participate in the program. Nor would federal, state, or local governments agree to share any of the costs. (To the contrary, state and local governments were *claimants*, demanding compensation of their own from BP.) And other potential contributors, such as Transocean and Halliburton, had expressed no interest in participating in the program. It did not have the time to commence complex heated negotiations with other companies about contributing to the GCCF. That would come later, after the new compensation program was up and running and claimants were being paid. Immediate compensation was deemed critical. No, it was BP, and BP alone, that would shoulder the entire financial burden of the GCCF, including my own pay. And it was prepared to do so.

But all of these reasonable arguments left unanswered the question: How could I be compensated by BP and still assert my independence? I turned to Judge Weinstein for advice. Creative and thoughtful as always, he suggested that an expert in legal ethics be retained to review and approve my formal relationship with BP. He also urged a second step, that I find a credible national figure who would issue an opinion letter stating in no uncertain terms that my compensation was reasonable and appropriate under the circumstances. These two letters would not protect me from all criticism, but they would go a long way in responding to the anticipated critics waiting in the wings.

I first turned to Professor Stephen Gillers, a national expert in legal ethics at New York University School of Law. Gillers carefully reviewed my unique relationship to BP as established by the company and the Obama administration. He reached a detailed, professorial conclusion: "As the administrator of the GCCF, you (including Feinberg Rozen) are not acting on behalf of a client, nor are you representing a client. Indeed, a nonlawyer could act as administrator of the GCCF without engaging in the unauthorized practice of law as routinely defined. And of course the GCCF is not a law firm and not authorized to practice law. . . .

"The fact that BP has an interest in the success of the GCCF does not make you its agent or its lawyer. Nor does the fact that BP is paying you for your services do so. While payment to a lawyer can be some evidence of a professional relationship with the payer, payment is neither sufficient by itself nor necessary to create an attorney-client relationship."

For the second opinion commenting on my specific compensation package, I turned to the former US attorney general, Michael B. Mukasey, who had also served as chief judge of the federal court in Manhattan. Mukasey and I had worked together as assistant US attorneys decades earlier, and had occasionally crossed paths since then. But we were hardly close friends. And as Judge Weinstein noted, his previous service as attorney general in the Bush administration would be an added plus in responding to political barbs from Republican officials.

Mukasey, now in private practice, was willing to review my compensation and prepare a formal opinion letter. He subsequently issued two letters, the first in October 2010, when I negotiated a flat legal fee of $850,000 per month for my law firm, and a second in March 2011, when BP agreed to raise the monthly retainer to $1.25 million. In both cases, Mukasey was clear and convincing in endorsing the reasonableness of the compensation:

> The Firm remains unrivaled in its experience, ability and reputation for claims work and is uniquely qualified to administer the GCCF, the largest fund in American history. . . . Statistics alone fail to capture the difficulty of the assignment. . . . In sum, the Firm remains unique in its qualification for the assignment, and the assignment remains unprecedented. . . . In light of this and of the matters set forth in our Initial Memorandum [of October 8, 2010], we have concluded that a flat fee of $1,250,000 per month through 2011 is reasonable.

The Gillers and Mukasey letters would not, of course, end the ongoing debate over my independence. But they offered sound, credible evidence that I was not merely a shill for BP. I carried these two letters in my suit pocket, ready to offer them up whenever I was accused of being BP's lackey.

I had learned a valuable lesson in administering the 9/11 fund: the importance of face-to-face meetings with claimants, engaging them directly both individually and collectively. Town hall–type meetings had been essential to the success of the 9/11 fund—as they had been for Agent Orange and the Hokie Spirit Memorial Fund. But this strategy had a very different result when applied to the GCCF.

To make up for the inevitable early delays in setting up the compensation program, I felt it only reasonable to visit the Gulf and confront any criticism head-on. Local citizens expected—were entitled—to visit with me on their home turf, to meet the public face of the claims program. They needed an opportunity to vent, criticize, argue, demand, implore, and seek compensation for their damages. I knew that many claimants would appreciate my local appearances in unfriendly environments. Even as I was battered with criticism, I would achieve some degree of credibility, even some admiration, in my choice to meet with fishermen in Louisiana, condo owners in Alabama, hoteliers in Florida, and restaurant owners in Mississippi.

Over the first six months of the GCCF program, I visited the Gulf just about every week, holding town hall meetings in the communities directly affected by the oil spill in Alabama, Florida, Louisiana, and Mississippi. Each meeting would last a few hours and I would attend as many as five or six meetings in one day, barnstorming from town to town and parish to parish to spread the word and urge the locals to file a claim.

Yet I found that these meetings—involving neighbors, friends, and entire local communities—did not necessarily assuage anger so much as compound it. The meetings reinforced each individual's determination to speak to power, to demand collectively what they would be reluctant to request in a private meeting. Those shouting the loudest received the most applause and encouragement. What developed was a type of "group think" and community reinforcement.

It was an interesting phenomenon. I would arrive at a local Louisiana parish, a town in Alabama, or a city in Florida. As many as five hundred local citizens would attend, often jammed into a school, church, or city hall auditorium. I first explained how the GCCF worked, how claimants should apply for compensation, and what was expected in the way of proof. My comments offered claimants a primer in how to get paid.

I then invited questions from the audience. The initial speakers would quietly explain their tales of woe, how the oil spill had affected their lives and how uncertain they were about the future. But as I recognized speaker after speaker, the anger grew and the frustration mounted. It usually reached a crescendo within fifteen minutes, with the audience shouting, "Pay him! Why won't you listen to her?! You're just working for BP!" Entire communities had their eyes on the prize: $20 billion ready to be distributed immediately.

I became a human piñata; every conceivable type of criticism was directed at me. Individual speakers would often begin a focused talk using notes or an outline but soon would meander into explanations as to why the spill caused their divorce, compelled the breakup of families, or led to tragic changes in "our way of life." It was as if the speakers simply wanted an opportunity to vent; they often spoke past me and directly to their neighbors.

The criticisms gradually developed a pattern; even before I arrived at a town hall meeting I knew exactly what to expect and how to respond. The complaints usually fell into one of five categories:

- Inconsistent awards: "Mr. Feinberg, my neighbor and I are waiters in the same restaurant. You gave her $20,000 but only gave me $10,000. What do you have against me? Why don't you like me?" My response: "Your neighbor reported income of $20,000 on her last tax return; you reported only $10,000. I can't compensate you for more than you would have earned."
- Delays in processing claims: "Mr. Feinberg, I am a fisherman. I filed my claim three months ago and I still haven't received a penny from the GCCF. Why are you sitting on my claim?" My response: "Because when you filed your claim, the only proof you offered was a fisherman's license. You gave us absolutely no evidence of financial damage attributable to the oil spill. When you send it, we will process the claim."
- Lack of transparency: "Mr. Feinberg, I asked for $50,000; the GCCF only sent me a check for $10,000. I have no idea why. The GCCF has not provided me any explanation for the difference." My response: "Yes it has, both in writing and when you visited the local claims office and received an explanation. But you don't like the answer. So, you shoot the messenger, ignoring the message."

- Absence of generosity: "Mr. Feinberg, BP promised to make us 'whole.' You are not doing this. You are trying to save money for BP. I received just 10 percent of what I requested. You must be getting paid by BP depending upon the money you saved." My response: "Wrong. The GCCF is being as generous as possible. Billions of dollars are being paid now to eligible claimants. But your individual claim is deficient or based on overly optimistic assumptions about future financial success. And my own compensation has nothing to do with the number of claims processed or the amounts being paid."
- Insensitivity to cultural differences: "Mr. Feinberg, you work in Washington. You cannot possibly understand how we do business down here. For generations, a handshake has been sufficient. The GCCF should recognize this." My response: "The business culture in the Gulf may be unique. But I cannot pay claims based on a handshake. I do not need extensive documentation or proof, but I need something that corroborates your claim."

Most of my critics (not all) were well intentioned and sincere in their belief that their future livelihood was now in jeopardy. They viewed the GCCF as their lifeline to economic security. GCCF payments would point the way. Elected officials played into these same fears and hopes. There was a direct correlation between political grandstanding and local citizen discontent.

In Alabama, Congressman Jo Bonner led the way, publicly upbraiding me: "The GCCF has been a dismal failure. There appears to be no improvement on the horizon. Consistency and transparency remain problematic. . . . It's a monster that's been created by this administration with the promise of making the people whole." Governor Bob Riley took second place: "The claims process designed and operated by Ken Feinberg unfairly manipulates the claims of innocent and powerless Alabamians in order to reduce the ultimate liability of BP, the company responsible for this disaster." Mayor Tony Kennon of Orange Beach was a close third: "Feinberg is not independent of BP."

In Florida, Chief Financial Officer Alex Sink, running for governor, viewed the GCCF as a perfect target for criticism in a close election race. "In my opinion, the GCCF rules must be rewritten in favor of those who were harmed by the catastrophe, as opposed to those who caused it." And outgoing Florida Attorney General Bill McCollum maintained a constant barrage of criticism: "The emergency payment protocol and claims process provided by Ken Feinberg last Friday appear to fall far short . . . and may well hamper injured parties as they seek to be made whole. . . . Despite repeated attempts by my office and many others in the Gulf Coast to assist Mr. Feinberg in drafting a Protocol that conforms to the requirements of OPA, Mr. Feinberg has consistently ignored our suggestions."

In Louisiana, Senator David Vitter was in a class by himself: "If my office was able [to] discover your empty promises in Louisiana, one can only guess the extent of your hollow rhetoric throughout the Gulf." But in his ongoing zeal to criticize, the junior senator from Louisiana made a textbook political error. Senator Kennedy taught me lesson one about local constituent service: never come to the public aid of a specific individual constituent unless you know all the facts and the underlying nature of the problem. Senator

Vitter ignored this first principle of constituent service. He sent me a letter expressing outrage at the GCCF's failure to process and pay the claims of seven named Louisiana citizens and immediately released it to the press:

> I would appreciate your not making empty promises to Louisianans, then making an empty promise to me before a committee hearing in the United States Senate, then hiding behind confidentiality, then providing an incomplete list to my office, all in an effort to hide behind the fact that your personal promises at the town hall meetings were meaningless. . . .
>
> ENCLOSURE: addendum list of people who stood up and voiced their concerns at your town hall meetings.

The senator had laid down this gauntlet in a very public fashion. Fortunately, I did have the data and could defend myself with the facts the senator had neglected to check. I immediately instructed the GCCF staff to review the status of these seven specific claims. Armed with the ammunition I needed, I responded publicly to Senator Vitter by posting my own letter on the GCCF website:

> Senator, I have reviewed all seven claims referenced in your Memorandum. I provide the following information in response to each of these inquiries while maintaining my commitment to the confidentiality of the claimants' personal information:
>
> • One claimant had an individual emergency Advance Payment denied because the individual claim overlapped with a simultaneous business claim that had already been paid.

Additionally, the documentation demonstrated that the claimant was a salaried employee who had suffered no reduction in salary during the Emergency Advance Payment period. She was so notified on January 6, 2011. The claimant's Interim claim is now under review and the claimant was notified on January 31, 2011 that documentation is required.

- One business submitted a request for an Emergency Advance Payment in an amount 2.5 times the business's total gross sales as reflected in the 2009 business tax return. The claimants were so notified in December of 2010. One of the claimants submitted income documentation consisting solely of a letter from her mother as the business owner; but the letter detailed individual earnings in excess of the business's total 2009 gross sales as reported in the submitted documentation.

- One claimant mentioned in your Memorandum has already received almost $1 million in an Emergency Advance Payment. But the claimant has yet to file either an Interim or Final claim for his business.

- One claimant you mention was denied an Emergency Advance Payment because of lack of documentation.

- Another claimant sought an Emergency Advance Payment in an amount that greatly exceeded the claimant's entire reported income for each of the two preceding years. The claimant has yet to file an Interim or Final claim, a prerequisite for GCCF consideration.

- In your Memorandum you mention a claimant who "finally got 1% of his claim [paid] in the amount of $54K."

The claimant received 13% of the amount sought, not 1%. The claimant was notified on February 7, 2011, and again on March 5, 2011, that certain specific missing documents will be required to process the Final claim.

• Another claimant mentioned in your Memorandum was denied an Emergency Advance Payment because of lack of documentation. The claimant's tax returns reported her occupation as "housewife" without any reference to her role, if any, in the business. The amount requested by her husband is approximately 250% of the gross income he previously reported from commercial fishing. . . .

Senator . . . I will not pay amounts that are wildly at odds with the claimant's prior year income documentation, nor will I pay undocumented claims.

Thereafter, Senator Vitter stopped publicly criticizing the GCCF.

In Mississippi, Attorney General Jim Hood, in a tight race for re-election, and a favorite of the trial lawyers suing BP, was a consistent, ongoing critic (and remains so to this day). No effort by the GCCF to address his daily criticisms had any impact. He was determined to politicize the entire debate. Hood had no Gulf Coast equal when it came to attacking both the GCCF and me personally. At one time he stated, "It is my continued belief that the failure to achieve the level of transparency and independent review promised in that [Escrow] Agreement has led to much confusion by claimants and has eroded public confidence in the integrity of the claims process. . . . Currently the public does not perceive the process as fair. . . . Given the number of complaints lodged against the GCCF by Mississippi claimants, I am compelled to conduct an investigation."

Hood then went one step further. He held his own town hall meetings and offered to assist any Mississippi claimants who formally authorized him to review their individual GCCF files. Hood received 155 authorizations, and he demanded complete access to all of them. The GCCF complied.

We never heard another word from him about any of these 155 claims.

Fortunately, not all elected officials jumped on the critical bandwagon. Some took the high road, acknowledging, at least privately, "Ken, you have one tough job. You won't hear criticism from me— or praise, either. It is all politics. Don't take it to heart." Senators Jeff Sessions and Richard Shelby of Alabama, Governors Charlie Crist and Rick Scott of Florida, Senator Mary Landrieu and Attorney General Buddy Caldwell of Louisiana, and Senators Thad Cochran and Roger Wicker of Mississippi all laid low, urging me forward and offering private words of encouragement.

But more than any other politician, Mississippi governor Haley Barbour gets my vote as a profile in courage. Testifying before a House Congressional Committee assessing the Gulf recovery efforts post–oil spill, Barbour was asked what he thought of the GCCF and its ongoing effort to compensate claimants. Expecting a broadside attack directed at the GCCF and a gratuitous swipe at the Obama administration, committee members must have been surprised by the governor's answer:

> I'm a recovering lawyer, OK? Do I know that a judge has ruled
> that the Gulf Coast compensation facility, whatever it's called,

that that is not truly independent of BP, and that may legally, technically be right. I think they are trying to do a good job. We don't get many complaints in Mississippi. They're doing something that's complicated, and I will say this about it. It is sure better than having to litigate all this, where people wouldn't get their money for years and years and years, and the trial lawyers would get half the money. So it is a long way from perfect, just like what I do is a long way from perfect. But I think it is better than the alternative of litigation. And as I say, we have cases that are difficult cases where people are not satisfied. But we really don't get many complaints, and we've been paid—Mississippi companies, people have been paid about 340 [million dollars], $350 million.

This was a rare and gratifying public admission that the GCCF was doing a difficult job well.

I was also amused by, and grateful for, a joint letter that Senators Vitter, Cochran, and Wicker sent to President Obama and released to the press early in 2011. Despite all the criticism I was receiving in the Gulf, they were concerned that I would resign as GCCF administrator to be appointed by the president to design and administer the new September 11th Victim Compensation Fund that Congress had enacted during the 2010 lame-duck session. Their letter implicitly acknowledged that much of the criticism already directed at me was unjustified; in any event, they wanted to make sure I stayed the course:

We request that the administration of the Gulf Coast Claims Facility not be burdened by the selection of Mr. Feinberg to administer the recently enacted 9/11 health compensation fund. If Mr. Feinberg is to administer the 9/11 fund we recommend that his appointment not move forward until all his work in the Gulf is complete. It is of utmost importance that the Gulf Coast individuals and businesses impacted by the Deepwater Horizon oil spill receive the full focus and consideration of the Gulf Coast Claims Facility through the completion of its chartered responsibilities.

Each senator's individual press release publicizing the letter went further:

Too often we have to fight to make sure the people of the Gulf Coast get fair treatment. . . . Mr. Feinberg should be given the opportunity to fully compensate those who suffered damages. [Senator Wicker]

I'm disappointed that Mr. Feinberg wouldn't definitively tell me while testifying in a committee hearing that he won't leave his critically important post until the job was done. It is my hope that as more of our colleagues join in calling for this commitment, he will see the importance of seeing the job through. [Senator Vitter]

I am concerned that interfering with the administration of the claims process at this point would be a setback and unnecessarily disrupt the work to help those hurt by the Deepwater Horizon tragedy. . . . I urge the President to allow Mr. Feinberg to keep his focus on the timely and fair processing of claims under the oil spill compensation program. [Senator Cochran]

Eventually, after months of repeated visits to the Gulf, I curtailed my travel schedule. Once the GCCF had proven its bona fides by paying billions of dollars to thousands of claimants, I knew that additional town hall meetings would be counterproductive, that they would serve only to provide a public forum for citizens who either did not have a valid claim or could not prove their damages. Judge Weinstein said it best: "Get the money out and stop the visits. You have paid the eligible claimants. You cannot satisfy the rest." My regular Gulf visits came to an end.

I made at least one big mistake in visiting the Gulf: I overpromised—something you should never do in administering a compensation program involving vulnerable, fragile people. In meeting after meeting during the first weeks of the GCCF, I made the ridiculous public pledge that "the GCCF will pay eligible individual claimants within forty-eight hours and eligible businesses within one week." Talk about a self-inflicted wound! Underestimating the volume and complexity of the claims, I promised what I could not possibly deliver. As a result, the GCCF was immediately placed on the defensive, failing to send out—as promised by the administrator himself—thousands of expected checks during the program's first few weeks. It would take months to recover from my gaffe.

Sadly, I also was unable to secure the support and cooperation of the trial lawyers, especially the lead attorneys in the huge oil spill litigation pending before federal Judge Carl J. Barbier in New Orleans. It's not surprising that this was the case. Although the trial bar had been instrumental in the ultimate success of the 9/11 fund, representing thousands of claimants pro bono, the BP oil spill was a different story. BP was the ready-made target for good old-fashioned, take-no-prisoners, deep-pocket litigation. The prospect of billions of dollars in punitive and compensatory damages—and hundreds of millions of dollars in legal fees—whetted the appetite of lawyers eager to represent thousands of innocent clients demanding retribution. And all in the name of the public interest—bringing a reckless oil company to heel.

Only one obstacle threatened the big payday: the GCCF. It had the potential to crash the party by offering billions of dollars to hundreds of thousands of potential plaintiffs. It stood as a clear alternative to the existing tort system. Every claim the GCCF paid meant one less lawsuit. So the GCCF was the enemy, a conspicuous alternative to the time-honored American way of resolving disputes in the courtroom.

Lawyer opposition was, therefore, understandable. But it wasn't all about legal fees. Trained in law school to view the adversary system as an almost sacred rite—the rule of law vindicated by lawyers advocating for their clients, with judges and juries determining the outcome—I recognized the inherent tension between the courtroom system and the GCCF. The new compensation program was a direct affront to everything trial lawyers learn and practice. They had a good-faith disagreement with the very idea of a GCCF. But in a real sense, they had chosen the wrong target. I was implementing an agreement entered into by others: the Obama administration and BP. Lawyers' gripes were better directed at the president and his Justice Department. But since I was the one person selected to make the proposal a reality, I braced myself for the onslaught.

Immediately after being appointed administrator, I met with a handful of the key trial lawyers preparing to litigate. I explained that the GCCF was a one-of-a-kind political response by the Obama administration to the Hurricane Katrina recovery fiasco in New Orleans that posed no long-term threat to the trial bar. Besides, plenty of innocent victims in the Gulf would actually prefer the courtroom.

But my overtures were quickly brushed aside. These lawyers— leaders among their brethren—would give no quarter in opposing the GCCF as a threat to their professional way of life. There would be no peace treaty. They would attack both the messenger and the message.

I also sought the help of the very same organizations that had stood shoulder to shoulder with me in designing and administering the 9/11 fund: the American Bar Association and the American Association for Justice. They cautiously expressed support "in principle," but their lawyer members would not countenance any type of meaningful active assistance. The organized bar was conflicted. It wanted to help, and acknowledged my credibility, but fearful of lawyer constituent criticism, it balked, hesitating to come forward with some type of comprehensive lawyer pro bono assistance program. It wavered while testing the political winds and ultimately declined to step forward. It would observe, not participate.

Fortunately, the trial bar was not monolithic. Scores of lawyers, unhappy with anticipated litigation that would drag on for years or even decades, and not part of the inner circle directing the lawsuits, threw in their lot with the GCCF. Many would be labeled as traitors to the cause, ostracized and drummed out of the club. They would not be permitted to participate in planning and executing the complex trial in New Orleans. Nor would they benefit from the legal fees the trial would generate. Most important, once excluded from the elite trial lawyer club, they would continue to be persona non grata when it came to any subsequent complex trials requiring joint plaintiff lawyer cooperation and coordination. Once isolated, always isolated. These outcasts all made the same arguments when meeting with me: if the GCCF would make generous, speedy payments to their clients, the flow of cash would provide the instant credibility the GCCF so desperately needed. But the fund would have to earn their trust. "Show me the money" was their call to arms.

I readily agreed to work with them—and anybody else who filed a claim. The GCCF could not and would not show any type of preference for a select group of lawyers or claimants. Any type of perceived bias in processing claims would prove the death knell of the GCCF.

One step that profoundly shaped the GCCF's story was the extraordinary offer we made as soon as the fund opened for business: to make emergency payments to all eligible claimants *without condition*. For ninety days—August 23 through November 23, 2010—the GCCF offered immediate cash to all claimants who could document eligibility and damage. Claimants could be compensated without surrendering their right to sue BP or anybody else. In addition, those receiving GCCF money could opt to return again and again for additional interim compensation if they could prove their ongoing damage.

This Emergency Advance Payment (EAP) was, in effect, an unprecedented gift. No previous mass compensation program had made such an unconditional payment offer. The much-praised 9/11 fund had required all claimants to sign a release promising not to sue. Not so with the EAP. Nor would the EAP in any way be hindered by tangential issues, such as monetary contributions by other defendant companies, such as Transocean and Halliburton, insurance or tax liens, or lawyers' fees. The EAP ignored all of these potential booby traps in making a lump-sum payment to the claimant. Once it was received, the claimant, and the claimant alone, was responsible for coping with any such side issues.

The EAP was sound public policy. Gulf victims did confront an emergency in the months immediately following the oil spill. Better for us to err on the side of generosity and speed than to pose legal technicalities that would stand as obstacles to prompt payment. I knew that first impressions were the key to success. The fund's credibility depended on a flood of cash, not a trickle, promptly flowing to victims.

Experience had taught me the first lesson of compensation programs: action, not promises. The EAP was designed with this principle in mind.

But I also was well versed in another important lesson: once a claimant signs on to a payment program and becomes familiar with it, he is likely to stay with it. This is a subtle psychological, "devil you know" aspect of compensation. Claimants were convinced they knew all about the strengths and weaknesses of the conventional litigation system. It was part of everyday life. But it would take time for them to adapt to a totally new compensation alternative. The EAP gave them this time to adjust, to test the waters without risk or obligation. It imposed no conditions on the claimant (such as a promise not to sue), but once individuals filed a claim with the GCCF and were satisfied with its generosity and speed, they would return for additional money, this time accompanied by terms and conditions. The EAP was designed to be an effective round one, laying the foundation for ongoing success.

BP officials challenged my decision to create the EAP. They feared I was just inviting claimants to use GCCF money (BP's money!) to sue BP. But I would not yield: "Just watch. I know how claimants will respond. Give them time. You will see."

The EAP should have been a home run, both financially and politically. But on the political side, it was met with derision and disdain. Rolled out in the shadow of the earlier well intentioned but flawed BP payment program and announced at the same time that BP was continuing its national ad campaign promising to make Gulf residents whole, it met fierce, emotional, and unrelenting criticism: too many claims were being denied; too much proof was required; it took too long to get paid; and GCCF officials offered inadequate explanations for their decisions.

Even the Department of Justice ran for cover. Buffeted by political criticism emanating from Gulf Coast Congressmen issuing press releases on a weekly basis, Tom Perrelli sent me a pointed letter: "I continue to have concerns about the pace of the claims process. . . . It is critical that you pay the remaining legitimate and documented emergency claims quickly. . . . I urge you to take action so that the GCCF improves its performance."

And while one cadre of critics was demanding more liberal payment standards, BP was publicly warning me in a posted letter that there was absolutely no legal justification for the GCCF to pay compensation to hotels and restaurants located in the Florida Peninsula, hundreds of miles from the oil spill. "There are a number of claims involving businesses whose alleged losses are derivative and economically remote to the oil spill and thus do not satisfy OPA's causation requirements. . . . While BP respects and does not seek to interfere with the GCCF's independent resolution of claims, it is imperative that the GCCF's actions comport with OPA in its evaluation and resolution of economic loss claims."

The critics were piling on the GCCF from every angle. No one was happy—except those claimants who were getting paid by the GCCF.

During the ninety-day EAP period, we received an onslaught of claims from almost 450,000 individuals and businesses—by mail, in person, and online. To those individuals who requested a lawyer but could not afford one, the GCCF contracted with the highly respected Mississippi Center for Justice to provide pro bono legal assistance. We also agreed to reimburse all eligible claimants for the cost of retaining local accountants to help prepare assessments of damage. The GCCF hired additional local lawyers and claims reviewers to staff the claims offices and assist claimants in obtaining the necessary documentation to support their claims. The objective was simple: to convince claimants that their neighbors, well respected in the local community, were working directly for them in making the fund more accessible and friendly. The GCCF could be trusted.

Money poured from the GCCF—some $2.4 billion paid to more than 169,000 people in the first ninety days, all without any obligation. By any statistical objective measure, the EAP was a success.

Yet the criticism continued: "Pay more; pay faster; you promised. We are desperate. You are paying everybody else. Why not me? Stop working for BP."

Stunned by the ongoing attacks, the GCCF responded, loosening the eligibility and proof requirements even further and authorizing overly generous payments. We paid individuals and businesses who would have been laughed out of court: hotels far from oil-soaked beaches, restaurants miles from the shore, golf course groundskeepers, beer distributors, retail stores, waiters and busboys working in New Orleans, more than fifty miles from the spill.

BP shuddered at this generosity, claimants being paid without even surrendering their right to sue. They feared I was going way too far with my "independence."

The GCCF was whipsawed from every direction. Claimants and politicians clamored for more generosity; BP urged restraint. The perfect storm.

Biros and the team assembled in Washington buckled but did not break. In an effort to rally the troops and reinforce the program's credibility, I went toe to toe with my critics. I embarked on a road show, appearing frequently on national and regional talk shows and visiting local newspaper editorial boards. My message was simple and defiant: the GCCF was working as expected; the EAP amounted to "found money," an unprecedented "gift." I noted that in just the first ninety days, the GCCF had processed more claims than any other private claims facility in American history. There was simply no precedent. The GCCF constituted a unique experiment made possible by the president's demand that BP do the right thing. I urged all who would listen to contrast the EAP's speed and impact with the glacial progress of conventional litigation. And if the GCCF did make mistakes—inevitable in light of claims volume—it would acknowledge the errors, fix the problems, and true up the payments.

As the ninety-day EAP program came to an end on November 23, 2010, I was slowly winning the struggle with my most vocal critics. The numbers, of course, were on my side, evidence of success. But beyond the statistics, it became apparent that I was prevailing in the court of public opinion. It was only the Gulf region residents and their elected officials who were making all the noise. The rest of the country—including both the Congress and the administration—appeared satisfied with the GCCF's progress and the fact that the oil no longer posed any immediate threat to the region. This national silence spoke volumes.

But the volume of claims we'd received in the relatively short time period forced us to confront certain realities. Obviously, there would be some delay in processing so many claims. This was inevitable in a payment program that required time-consuming accounting review of each individual submission. Was the claimant eligible? Were tax returns and other documentary proof submitted? What damage calculations should be made? What financial assumptions should be accepted? Should claimants be afforded an opportunity to cure deficiencies in proof?

Treating all claimants alike by offering the same compensation regardless of individual circumstances made no sense. Such an approach would overpay thousands of claimants and shortchange others.

Nor could the GCCF simply accept at face value a claimant's wishful pie-in-the-sky compensation demands. The $20 billion would be exhausted in a matter of days. (One claimant made an urgent plea for $11 billion; another demanded all $20 billion himself.) If the GCCF approved all such requests regardless of corroboration, $200 billion would not be enough.

The volume of claims had other adverse consequences. Individual hearings—so essential to the success of the 9/11 fund—would be impractical for the GCCF. Almost 450,000 people were demanding immediate emergency cash. Under the circumstances, the right to be heard was at odds with requirements of speed and efficiency. With the 9/11 fund, we had the luxury of receiving a total of "only" about 7,500 claims in thirty-three months, and fewer than half of these individuals requested a hearing. The GCCF received more than that in a single day. Our inability to provide a tailored individual hearing to each and every claimant inevitably distanced the GCCF from the very people it sought to serve.

Although formal hearings were out of the question, I did add personnel to local offices to help claimants, and offered translators who would assist any claimant requesting help. This was a poor second to formal hearings. But at least it provided individuals a one-on-one opportunity to express their opinions. I wanted individual Gulf residents to believe they were not simply cogs in a bureaucratic machine, that each claim and each claimant were important to the GCCF. I never completely solved this problem, one that will continue to bedevil any effort at mass resolution of claims.

The volume of emergency payments also raised the specter of fraud. There will always be individuals who try to game the system by altering or forging tax returns, submitting false documents pertaining to employment, lying about their income and number of dependents, or asserting oil spill damage when there is none. It is one thing to try to take advantage of a generous payment program; wishful thinking is not criminal fraud. But when a claimant intentionally makes false statements on a claim form or alters federal tax returns or other official records, he or she crosses the line from stretching the truth to committing a felony.

Nothing can undercut the credibility of claims compensation more than evidence of fraud. Fortunately, during the administration of the September 11th Victim Compensation Fund, evidence of actual fraud was rare. Claims were limited, and all involved death or physical injury which could be documented easily by an official death certificate, accompanying medical records, airline passenger manifests, or Pentagon military files. Fewer than three dozen fraudulent claims were submitted to the 9/11 fund and all were turned over to the Department of Justice for prosecution.

But the GCCF process was different, both in quantity and quality. Instead of death and physical injury, we had to analyze documents offered as proof of lost wages and lost income. This proved fertile ground for fraudulent schemes, some crude and obvious, others more complex and ingenious. Some individuals doctored their tax returns by adding zeros to the income line, falsifying deductions, multiplying the number of dependents, or presenting a "tax return" that was never filed; other applicants submitted different versions of income statements and tried to explain away discrepancies between the income statements and income reported in federal tax returns; still others stated that their income tax returns were incorrect because their own tax preparers had attempted to do a "special deal" to avoid placing them in a higher income tax bracket. We heard from supposed restaurant workers who submitted fabricated paystubs, tax documents, and employment letters, ship captains who claimed income losses involving fictitious boats, and commercial fishermen who sent in fabricated deckhand verifications and tax records. And some claimants alleged the ownership of small businesses that were fabricated and managed through an elaborate system of mail drops and mail forwarding services.

To deal with fraud, the GCCF retained the services of Guidepost, a respected company with a long track record of conducting internal corporate investigations and uncovering evidence of business fraud. Guidepost became our GCCF antifraud unit. Suspicious claims were identified and targeted by one of our senior GCCF review teams. These claims were then sent to Guidepost for further review and local investigation. Guidepost would also investigate tips and leads disclosed by anonymous whistleblowers who telephoned the Department of Justice fraud hotline.

During the life of the program, the GCCF investigated over 17,000 suspicious claims and referred almost 4,000 of these to the Department of Justice for further investigation and, when appropriate, prosecution. Although this was a large number, it paled in significance to the total number of over 1 million claim filings. In my public defense of the GCCF, I constantly referenced the work of Guidepost and the determination of the GCCF to weed out fraud.

———

At the end of the ninety-day EAP period, the GCCF commenced phase two of the compensation program. The fund offered each eligible claimant a menu of three payment choices, without favoring or preferring any particular option:

Quick payment. This proved to be by far the most popular option. Any individual who had already received an emergency payment from BP or the GCCF could file a simple form without submitting any further documentation of damage and receive a check within two weeks for $5,000. Similarly, a business could quickly file and receive $25,000 from the GCCF.

Since BP or the GCCF had already evaluated the claim's merits during the earlier emergency phase, this option provided the claimant with ready additional cash. But claimants exercising this option had to sign a full release promising not to sue BP or any other businesses deemed responsible for the rig explosion; nor could the claimants return to the GCCF seeking additional compensation. In the year after the end of the EAP period, over 130,000 individuals and businesses accepted this quick-payment option, and the fund paid $1.3 billion in quick payments.

The ease and speed of the quick-payment option accounted for its popularity. So did the nature of the Gulf's underground economy, where tax returns and financial documentation were honored in the breach, making it hard for thousands of individuals and businesses to post the proof necessary for a larger payment. The quick-payment option was perfect for them.

Some paternalistic trial lawyers and local elected officials criticized this system. They said that claimants were not exercising a true free choice and that they were compelled by economic circumstances to accept the quick-payment monies being dangled in front of them by an opportunistic GCCF in exchange for an overly broad surrender of future rights.

Still, I defended this option. Where was there the slightest evidence that economic compulsion was at the heart of a claimant's decision to opt for a quick payment? Saying it didn't make it so. Gulf Coast residents knew what they were doing. They chose quick payment willingly and were within their rights to do so.

While the arguments played out in public, thousands of claimants rushed to accept the cash. Stunned BP officials watched with amazement. I again reminded BP officials why the earlier EAP made sense for both claimants and the company. No release had been necessary or warranted during the emergency phase; the goal was immediate compensation for victims. But once claimants became familiar and comfortable with the payment program and received their cash, they would return—by the thousands—hoping for additional compensation. This time the cash carried with it the obligation not to sue. BP applauded.

Interim payment. This second option was available to claimants who were uncertain about their financial future and were not prepared to sign any type of lawsuit release. Concerned about the spill's long-term effect on the fishing, shrimping, and oyster harvesting industries, as well as tourism and related retail businesses, they preferred a short-term payment while they continued to monitor recovery efforts in the Gulf. This allowed them to document their past quarterly damage while maintaining their right both to sue and to return to the GCCF for additional quarterly payments if the damage continued. At some point in the future, a full release and final payment might be in order, but for now the risk-free interim system was attractive.

More than 35,000 individuals and businesses opted for interim payments, receiving an aggregate total of $495 million in just the first year. In effect, this was the EAP all over again, an opportunity to receive GCCF compensation without obligation. Of course, these individuals were required to document their ongoing damage each quarter. This would not be easy. All signs pointed to accelerated biological, environmental, and economic recovery in the Gulf. BP and the US Coast Guard had done a remarkable job in containing and recovering the oil spewing from the damaged rig. Nature had helped, with the warm waters and climate apparently resulting in further evaporation of the oil slick. The economy continued to improve; any remaining financial uncertainty could not easily be traced to the oil spill, as opposed to the general economic downturn in the region (and the rest of the nation). The Gulf states and the Environmental Protection Agency were touting the safety and health of fishing stock. Meanwhile, BP was paying millions of dollars to state and local governments to promote tourism. Elected officials were photographed eating Gulf shrimp and oysters, and urging vacationing tourists to return to pristine beaches. For much of the nation, the oil spill was fast becoming yesterday's news.

But I fully appreciated the financial uncertainty that troubled thousands of individuals and businesses in the Gulf. The signs of economic recovery were promising but the crystal ball remained murky. Elected officials and, of course, the trial lawyers, highlighted this interim payment option, urging claimants (who could later become lawsuit plaintiffs) to take the money, preserve their litigation rights, and hedge against future uncertainty.

I was accused of downplaying the advantages of interim payments, and the GCCF was criticized for deliberately delaying the payment of interim claims and demanding more documentation than was necessary. The facts showed otherwise. There was no effort to delay interim payments or to demand more onerous proof than needed. The critics ignored an important aspect of human nature: claimants' natural reluctance to make repeated submissions to the GCCF to receive compensation. Experience has taught me that, the paternalism of government officials and lawyers notwithstanding, claimants want closure. It is unsettling and troublesome to be reminded over and over again about tragedy. So although thousands of claimants would opt for an interim payment, many thousands more would decide to move on, close the oil spill chapter, and look to the future. The choice was theirs.

Final payment. This option was available for eligible claimants who wanted to be done once and for all with the oil spill. It was clearly the most generous option—and the riskiest. If claimants could document their past, present, and *future* damage, they would receive a single lump-sum check to cover it all. In exchange, they had to relinquish their right to return to the GCCF and sign a full release promising not to sue.

But how to value future risk? There was the rub. Predicting the Gulf's future not only was a problem for claimants but also posed a huge challenge to the GCCF. All final payments had to include a "future recovery risk factor," compensation for the time it would take for Gulf fishing grounds to be restored, shrimping and oyster harvesting to be back to normal, and tourists to return for vacation. But how long? How much?

The GCCF sought advice from various independent experts. It also retained the services of Analysis Research Planning Corporation (ARPC)—a firm with a national reputation for economic modeling, data collection, and statistical prediction—to issue a report documenting the region's financial future. Professor Wes Tunnell, Jr. at the Texas A&M Harte Research Institute for Gulf of Mexico Studies, one of the nation's foremost marine biology authorities, also weighed in with his opinions as to when the Gulf would return to pre-spill seafood harvest status. So did federal and state environmental officials.

After reviewing all of the evidence, we agreed with ARPC that it was "reasonable"—but by no means certain—that Gulf resources and the local Gulf economy would return to normal by the end of 2013. Accordingly, we announced a final-payment formula that consisted of documented 2010 losses multiplied by a "future recovery risk factor" of two. Those eligible claimants choosing this option would receive a check covering all losses through 2013.

Oyster harvesters posed a special problem. The oysters and the oyster beds were damaged or destroyed primarily by fresh water pumped into the Gulf to disburse the oil from affected areas. The oyster industry confronted greater additional risk. So the GCCF provided eligible oyster claimants a future recovery risk factor of four, encompassing predicted damage through 2015.

The GCCF braced for the predictable reaction. Sure enough, our critics attacked the future factor as being insufficient. Some said it should be six, eight, or even ten times 2010 losses. They claimed I was merely trying to save money by underestimating the uncertainties of a depressed Gulf region economy.

But the GCCF had relied on a comprehensive array of expert opinions, both public and private; economic recovery by 2013 was indeed reasonable. My argument was also enhanced by the fact that BP itself went public in its loud opposition to the "future recovery risk factor." It asserted that the GCCF was being much too generous, that the Gulf Region was quickly returning to normal. It urged us to reduce the future recovery risk factor to less than one year, reflecting the limited ongoing harm caused by the oil spill. But I rejected its entreaties.

I did promise that the GCCF would continue to monitor the Gulf and reserved the right to modify the recovery factor, up or down, as events unfolded. Nine months later, the GCCF would in fact offer the shrimp and crab industries in the Gulf the same four times future recovery risk factor as it originally had offered oyster harvesters. Projected increased risk for shrimpers and crabbers required the modification.

But second-guessing was guaranteed—whether by claimants or BP.

Most important, I reminded all who would listen that no claimant was required to opt for a final payment. If an individual believed that the final-payment calculation did not adequately protect against future risk, the claimant could select an interim payment and take a "wait and see" approach to the future. The interim-payment option was always available, a type of safety valve for those who were not yet willing to gamble on their future.

In the first year of the final-payment option, more than 73,000 individuals and businesses accepted it—more than double the number who selected interim payments. What better evidence of the credibility of this option? And as the months went by, it became more and more apparent that individuals and businesses in the Gulf were acknowledging that the region was returning to normal, that documenting damage was becoming increasingly difficult, that the final-payment option was a way of encouraging people to move on.

As the end of 2011 approached, the GCCF was well on its way to accomplishing the objectives President Obama articulated in making the deal with BP. In the program's first sixteen months—weeks before the very first trial—the GCCF had already paid about $6.1 billion to well over 500,000 claimants. More than 97 percent of all claims filed with the GCCF had been "processed"; the remaining 3 percent constituted the most recent filings (with more than 1,500 new claims arriving each week). Despite this unprecedented onslaught of claims, the GCCF was current in evaluating all claims.

With the benefit of hindsight, it at least appears that, when it comes to private individual and business claims (as opposed to government claims and state and local Gulf cleanup costs), BP was more than generous in pledging $20 billion. The scale and impact of the disaster now seems to be much less than originally feared. BP and the US Coast Guard mounted a huge, largely successful, oil cleanup effort. Nature provided assistance. Warm temperatures helped dissolve much of the natural oil spewing from the damaged rig; the remainder was recovered by both Coast Guard and private vessels engaged in the cleanup operation. Even most of the pending government claims from Gulf states and local communities are for relatively modest sums. They encompass the hiring of additional personnel to assist in cleaning up oil soaked beaches or providing assistance to contractors and others involved in the cleanup effort. BP, not the GCCF, is responsible for evaluating and paying these government claims.

In creating the GCCF, and urging that it act independently from BP, both the Obama administration and the company were able, in effect, to compartmentalize the fallout from the spill, and direct any and all legitimate claims either to the GCCF or BP itself for payment. It is a perfect example of good government in action, of a creative and workable government/private company partnership. Now, almost two years since the tragedy, the all-in number for paying private and government claims, as well as local cleanup costs, appears to be less than half the $20 billion pledged by BP.

Of course, the final accounting is far from over.

Despite some ongoing criticism from Gulf residents and their elected officials, I believe that the unique experiment called the GCCF vindicated the president's commitment to come to the rescue of Gulf Coast residents harmed by the environmental catastrophe. The statistics speak for themselves (as of March 9, 2012):

1,061,405 Claims Filed with the GCCF
EAP, quick-, interim-, and final-payment claims
(574,881 Claimants from fifty states and
thirty-eight foreign countries)

$6.139 Billion Paid
$2.5 billion—emergency claims
$3.5 billion—quick, interim, and final claims

169,203 Claimants Paid—emergency payments
128,172—quick payments
67,143—final payments
35,261—interim payments
420,430—claimants denied or filing claims deemed deficient

Even the clamor from the Gulf has subsided. As expected, most individuals and businesses have moved on, and Gulf elected officials have shifted their sights to other, more pressing matters.

Critics of the GCCF are running out of credible arguments. Only one remains: the demand that the Department of Justice authorize an independent audit of the GCCF. Desperate to find something—anything—that could tarnish our work (and with it, the Obama administration), critics have latched on to the idea of an open-ended search for some GCCF defect, error, or inconsistency. Longtime fund critics Jo Bonner, vice chair of the House subcommittee with appropriations authority over the Department of Justice, and Mississippi Attorney General Hood have tried making the case, generally relying on an appeal to "transparency," a label that has come to rival apple pie and motherhood as an unquestioned political shibboleth. Bonner even made sure that his demand became part of the new law appropriating funds for the department: "To ensure that the GCCF is operating in accordance with the letter and intent of existing law, and in a timely, transparent and consistent manner, the Committee directs the Department, in consultation with the Government Accountability Office (GAO), to identify an independent auditor to evaluate GCCF's claims determination methodologies and the qualifications of GCCF personnel."

I have never opposed the idea of an independent audit. In fact, it makes considerable sense, especially in light of the emergency circumstances creating the GCCF. Neither the Obama administration nor BP had any day-to-day oversight of GCCF decision-making. As signatories to the escrow agreement, they could monitor our work but not interfere. An independent audit not only would bring sunlight to the process, but it also would, I was convinced, vindicate our work.

I was not prepared to sign off on an audit conducted too early in the fund's life. It would be a mischievous distraction while the GCCF was trying to process thousands of emergency claims. Nor did I want to divert important resources to the audit. And I realized that any audit conducted in the glare of a political spotlight would invariably chill the zeal and single-mindedness of GCCF accountants and claims adjusters focused on processing claims.

The drumbeat of critics calling for an audit continued for a year. Finally, during the summer of 2011, I met with Attorney General Holder and Tom Perrelli and agreed that the time was ripe for an audit. The dollars distributed, the number of claims processed, and the fact that the GCCF was current with claims in the queue all pointed to a truly independent audit vindicating the fund's work. The attorney general sent me a letter formalizing our understanding:

> I note the GCCF's progress in the face of nearly one million claims filed and appreciate your efforts. The GCCF's work continues to be critical, and we will continue to hold it to the highest standards of efficiency, consistency, and customer service.
>
> At our meeting, we discussed concerns that I heard in the Gulf regarding the transparency of the process. This letter will confirm your conversation with Associate Attorney General Tom Perrelli, in which you agreed, as we discussed at our meeting, to an independent audit of the GCCF. We recognize, however, that the GCCF is continuing to get thousands of claims

per week, and that resolving those claims quickly and fairly should be its highest priority. Consequently, we will work with you to identify an appropriate time to commence such an audit before the end of the year, in a manner that will not disrupt the timely processing of claims.

The Department of Justice chose the auditor, BDO Consulting. The audit started in January 2012 and will conclude in April 2012.

One interesting fact has gone largely unnoticed by those critics calling for an audit. They maintain that the GCCF has been too inconsistent in determining eligibility and calculating damages and has not been sufficiently generous. Yet there is already a law on the books that allows official review of these cases. The OPA statute requires that any claimant unhappy with a GCCF determination should have the statutory right to ask the US Coast Guard to make an independent firsthand review of the claim. Indeed, some 1,612 claimants, both individuals and businesses, have already sought and received such a review. *And in every single instance, the Coast Guard has ultimately agreed with the GCCF's determinations.*

Furthermore, the Coast Guard itself has expressed the view in formal Senate hearings that the GCCF has gone above and beyond OPA. As a senior Coast Guard official stated:

The protocols that are out there—that BP and GCCF have been able to do—have actually been more inclusive than OPA requires. They can pay for personal injury. They can pay Emergency Advance Payments. [The Coast Guard] can't pay advance payments. Their final claims protocol will include prospective losses. [The Coast Guard] can't pay for speculative losses.

But some people in the Gulf hear what they want to hear. They are not assuaged. There must be a conspiracy involving the GCCF and the Coast Guard—and no amount of proof will convince them otherwise.

Critics such as Bonner and Hood point to the fact that the GCCF was established without a statute or a set of administrative rules promulgated by a government agency and published in the official Federal Register for all to read. They decry this situation as "lawless." But the critics ignore the unique emergency that gave rise to the agreement creating the GCCF. The $20 billion "handshake" did an end run around government bureaucracy and delay at a time when the public demanded speed. No question: there is a price to be paid when you short-circuit normal procedures in this way. But the September 11th Victim Compensation Fund was a clear precedent for the GCCF. Like the escrow agreement establishing the GCCF, it gave the special master broad authority to define his own operating procedures and principles. And in both instances the executive branch used this open-ended arrangement to deflect criticism and redirect it to the man in charge.

The plan worked. The details of compensation were left to me—along with any political controversy that might arise in the process. And I accepted the challenge.

Like the 9/11 fund, the GCCF is unlikely to be replicated. It is a one-off. This is unfortunate. When in our history has any other private company confronting potentially huge liabilities agreed to acknowledge responsibility within days and immediately post $20 billion to demonstrate its good faith to both victims and the public? Most businesses choose to delay accepting responsibility for years; it is the American way. Not BP. And I know of no precedent in which a private claim facility has been established to review and analyze more than 1 million claims, one by one, claim by claim.

Yet other companies confronting potential large legal liabilities might carefully consider the wisdom of the BP strategy: advance the necessary funds to attract potential courtroom adversaries; design and implement an alternative compensation program that highlights the advantages of speedy and generous compensation; invite resolution far from courtroom judges, juries, and lawyers; and resolve nearly all the claims through a purely private payment program that largely avoids direct government involvement.

At the same time, the genesis of the GCCF is unique—and admittedly troublesome. Despite all of its ambiguities and uncertainties, the September 11th Victim Compensation Fund at least was created by statute. Congress partnered the effort. But the GCCF is a unique hybrid, part public, part private. True, OPA required BP to step up and process claims, but the statute never anticipated a handshake deal between BP and a US president creating an independent claims facility. One can legitimately question whether this accelerated, abbreviated approach, delegating so much authority to one person, was the best way for the government to respond to the worst environmental disaster in American history. Or was it precisely because of the uniqueness of the tragedy that an innovative government response was required? The president certainly cannot be accused of failing to act with dispatch. The magnitude of the crisis required it.

The final chapter in this tragedy is now being written. The Obama administration and BP agreed to keep the GCCF in place until August 2013 in order to process pending and future claims. But in March 2012 the plaintiff lawyers in New Orleans reached a comprehensive class action settlement with BP, calling for an orderly transition from the GCCF to a new claims program to be administered under the auspices of Judge Barbier. If the proposed settlement is approved by the courts, as I hope it will be, the GCCF experiment will become history within the next few months.

The proposed settlement is interesting in a number of respects. First, despite all of the criticism directed at the GCCF by the trial lawyers, the new claims program will apparently continue to use the same exact services of BrownGreer, the Garden City Group, and PricewaterhouseCoopers. Feinberg Rozen, of course, will depart, but those companies so critical to the success of the GCCF will remain, proof positive that their GCCF achievements did not go unnoticed.

In addition, the new payment program will, like the GCCF, develop eligibility criteria, damage calculation methodologies, and proof requirements. But the new program will be under the jurisdiction of the federal court; it will not be a stand-alone outlier like the GCCF. It will, therefore, be similar to Judge Weinstein's Agent Orange payment program, with Judge Barbier ultimately overseeing its day-to-day operations.

The announced settlement agreement does promise some important substantive changes from GCCF payment rules. It plans to pay health-related claims—especially respiratory illnesses allegedly affecting oil clean-up workers and shore residents who inhaled oil fumes following the spill. (The GCCF paid millions of dollars to rig workers who suffered traumatic physical injuries as a result of the explosion but declined to pay respiratory claims citing the absence of both medical proof of causation and evidence of permanent physical disability.) The announcement also states that recreational subsistence claims—boat owners who could not enjoy a Sunday cruise in the Gulf, homeowners on the Gulf shore who suffered the inconvenience of inhaling oil odors and observing noisy BP and Coast Guard clean-up efforts—will be compensable. It remains to be seen whether these open-ended eligibility provisions will result in hundreds of thousands, even millions, of new claims brought by workers and Gulf residents seeking quick, convenient cash.

None of my prior assignments in designing and administering public compensation programs prepared me for the GCCF experience. The BP oil spill taught me new lessons. Without political consensus and bipartisan support, which I benefited from in my earlier work, it is much more difficult to achieve success and secure public approval. The key fundamental ingredient of *credibility* is called into question. Claimant confidence in the program begins to waver. Doubt festers. The administrator's personal integrity is questioned. The process for effectively processing claims and providing compensation is directly influenced by the surrounding political environment. Add to this the practical reality of reviewing more than 1 million claims in a timely fashion, and the challenges multiply. And when the admitted wrongdoer is front and center, promising to pay $20 billion or whatever is necessary to right the wrong, thousands of individuals have a ready answer to the question of who gets what: "We get it—all of it!"

I will readily defend the fund's success. The president's pledge to Gulf citizens has been redeemed in full. Billions of dollars have been paid to hundreds of thousands of individuals and businesses in record time. Public approval—nationally and, I believe, in the Gulf—has gradually been achieved. Thousands of lawsuits were avoided and the GCCF payment program paved the way for a comprehensive settlement of the remaining litigation in New Orleans.

In an important sense, therefore, I view the GCCF as my most significant achievement in light of the obstacles, the criticism, and the challenges. I take pride in the results. I rode out the perfect storm.

But I am in no rush to do it again.

EPILOGUE

"A Sense of Entitlement"

For more than twenty-five years, my professional life has been defined by disasters and tragedies. I have been asked by presidents, attorneys general, the secretary of the Treasury, the Congress, and judges to design and administer compensation programs aimed at alleviating the financial plight of innocent victims. I have been tasked with determining what corporate officials should earn. In so doing, I have learned firsthand how compensation and human nature interact, how they feed off each other. The decisions I have had to make would have been impossible without an understanding of how people react to tragedy, how they view compensation, and what they expect in receiving a check. In my work I benefit from neither a degree in divinity nor one in psychology or psychiatry. But these specialties come to the fore in trying to do justice, in attempting to compensate fairly.

Understanding the mind-set of those receiving compensation, their reaction to dollars-and-cents calculations, is critical to success.

I must stress that I am not the only one making decisions of this nature. Compensating victims of tragedy, providing pay packages to senior businessmen, and other such judgment calls are part of everyday life in our nation. Judges, juries, and corporate compensation committees make thousands of such decisions daily. So do federal and state regulatory agencies in dealing with diverse and complex subjects: health care, workers' compensation awards, social security payments, and other social entitlement programs. Even in the absence of time-honored tort litigation, compensation flows daily as an integral part of the modern American administrative state.

But all of these compensation decisions are made away from public scrutiny, part of the daily fabric of legal and commercial life. These need no explanation, at least no public explanation.

Once in a while, however, these decisions become highly visible. Pay becomes front-page news, usually in response to a national calamity. Sunlight is brought to bear on the subject. A public debate about the role of compensation in American society ensues. And some first principles are called into question.

In deciding who gets what in American society, money is almost always the vehicle of exchange. We simply assume this as an obvious feature of modern life. Public memorials may be erected to signify and symbolize loss; a formal government or private apology may follow an admission of wrongdoing; and emotional, legal, and educational assistance may be a worthy substitute for cash in certain situations. In other countries, Truth and Reconciliation Commissions have been established by law to provide citizens a formal opportunity to express sorrow and atone for the past. As alternatives to cash payment, barter and indenture have served as forms of compensation, especially in earlier colonial times. But when we discuss how to compensate innocent victims of wrongdoing or determine the value of corporate employment, Americans rely upon money. It's a natural outgrowth of our free market, capitalist history.

Money is also integral to our legal system. Not only does it provide material help to the innocent, but its loss is designed to deter others from committing similar wrongs. And in an important sense, the exchange of money constitutes public acknowledgment of injustice and loss. It can serve as an expression of citizen support, the community standing as one with the victim.

But with cash as the primary form of compensation, it is still necessary to decide who should receive the money, under what circumstances, and how much. These questions become particularly difficult to answer when they must be resolved in the midst of very public debate. The innocent victim of an automobile accident may receive thousands of dollars in damages by judge and jury. But this transfer of cash, made each day in courtrooms throughout our nation, is done without fanfare, without media attention. It is everyday news, ordinary happenstance. It is one person, standing alone, receiving compensation for wrongs suffered. In such cases, society quietly fulfills its obligation to each of its citizens.

So, too, with the executive who is compensated for work performed. His paycheck is rarely newsworthy. It is a free market transaction between employer and employee. It does not demand public inspection or reaction. It is part of a private contract, basic to our economic system.

But the equation changes dramatically when the public spotlight shines on these compensation decisions, when citizens demand to know who gets what. This attention results from very public tragedies that are front-page news: a terrorist attack, an oil spill, a deranged gunman, a financial meltdown. The public's interest is aroused. Whether because of public pressure, political expediency, a legitimate sense of outrage, or a combination of these and other factors, policy makers must respond. Though existing law may be capable of addressing these tragedies, in the context of a mounting public uproar, its machinations seem too complex, too time-consuming, too inefficient, or too uncertain. This doesn't mean that the law is incapable of attending to compensation issues, or that some tragedies are more deserving than others. It is simply the case that sometimes the public's outrage demands more—part of the nature of democracy. The result is the same: we need to do something different this time, to craft a new out-of-the-box policy. Business as usual will not do.

The public's interest grows all the more acute when special funds are created to pay victims, or when corporate officials deemed responsible for a financial crisis are called on the carpet. This is not ordinary, not everyday, not mainstream. Now compensation decisions take on a whole new life. What is usually private becomes very public. And it is not just one victim, or one CEO, who becomes the subject of public interest. Now thousands of victims or scores of corporate leaders are affected by the crisis. A collective focus zeroes in on individual considerations of compensation, damage, or pay. An often passionate debate ensues, not only among the public but also among the victims and corporations themselves.

Human nature is a key element of this debate. Special compensation programs aimed at a select few inevitably lead to heightened expectation: "This program was created for me. I am entitled to be paid. I deserve compensation. I am worthy." What results is a *sense of entitlement,* a resolute belief that the dollars to be exchanged are justified. Both the innocent victim of wrongdoing or tragedy and the corporate officer working for a pay package believe—in absolute good faith—that they are entitled, that they deserve, that they have every right to demand and expect.

This leap in thinking is easy to understand. To the recipient of compensation, the public has already acknowledged the legitimacy of this sense of entitlement by establishing a special compensation program in the first place; fellow citizens and lawmakers have validated the merit of their own individual claims. Similarly, designated corporate executives are only too ready to mount the soapbox and defend the appropriateness of their pay: "The government expects me to justify my worth. Great! I will do so."

As administrator of these programs, I am expected to deliver the goods—to pay the claims, to make victims whole, to ratify a corporate compensation package. If I fail to do so, I am accused of demeaning both the claim and the claimant. On the other hand, if I ask for evidence of eligibility, documentation of damage, or comparative corporate pay practices, I am accused of being a pettifogger and micromanager, nickel-and-diming worthy individuals and reducing them to figures in a ledger.

Compounding the problem is the fact that *everybody counts other people's money.* It is a natural human trait. Comparison shopping is the rule. The absolute yields to the relative. And it gets very personal. "Rough justice" in establishing these special compensation programs—the pursuit of the greatest good for the greatest number—means very little to each individual expecting fair treatment from the administrator or special master. Their own individual claim is the most important claim in the world, and their own compensation package is all that matters. An award calculation that, for perfectly valid and appropriate reasons, is less than their next-door neighbor's award can trigger outrage: "What do you have against me? Why are you questioning the value of my claim? Why are you paying others more than me?"

The problem is also exacerbated when there are only finite dollars to distribute. Counting other people's money becomes automatic and self-serving. The Peter/Paul principle is immediately invoked: "You must be paying me less to make sure that other claimants get more." No wonder that as an administrator, I always prefer having unlimited funds to work with—one less emotional issue to deal with in meeting with claimants.

In these circumstances conspiracy theories are rife. Again, this is part of human nature. Dark, mysterious forces are alleged to be at work undermining the claims process: the administrator is in BP's pocket; he is merely Judge Weinstein's agent, or a stooge for the university, or the mayor of New York; he is a secret populist, a former aide of Senator Kennedy, determined to reduce corporate pay as part of an insidious scheme of class warfare.

And the trial lawyers can usually be counted on to fuel such suspicions. This is perfectly understandable. Trained in the traditions of the law, determined to vindicate individual rights in the courtroom with the help of judge and jury, these lawyers have little use for any new compensation program that minimizes their central role in securing justice. I frequently hear the argument that for trial lawyers this behavior is all about their financial livelihood. There is, of course, something to this, but not much. Trial lawyer opposition runs much deeper and is more profound. To these lawyers, the GCCF, for example, is "compensation on the cheap," with inadequate procedural protections, few if any checks and balances, and insufficient payments. They find it antidemocratic, in compensating the few rather than the many, and altogether too dependent on the discretion of a single administrator.

I always hope that reason will prevail, that the facts will trump emotion. The unique compensation initiatives I have administrated are exceedingly rare. Lawyer hyperbole notwithstanding, they pose no threat to conventional methods of determining pay and damages. They are stand-alone public policy creations, tailored to meet the moment. And ironically, if the trial lawyers would lower their voices and their heated criticism, there is a fair amount of merit to their arguments.

Special compensation programs do raise fundamental questions about fairness. Why do some victims of life's tragedies receive a fast-track ticket to quick cash, when other innocent victims do not qualify or must patiently wait their turn to gain access to the courtroom? Why this special treatment for a select few? Conversely, the top twenty-five corporate executives in the seven companies subject to the pay czar's commands may understandably question why they have been singled out for special treatment; what about the top fifty executives, or the top one hundred? And why only seven companies instead of seventy or seven hundred?

These are troublesome questions. In our society, which frowns on elitism and promotes the concept of equal protection under the law, there is unease in promulgating special rules for special people. And it must be admitted that, at least in this sense, these programs *are* inherently inequitable. All special compensation programs confront this same tension: special rules for a select few.

This is why these compensation programs are exceedingly rare—and should remain so.

I have been asked to design and administer one on just five occasions during the past twenty-eight years—a rate that hardly suggests a burgeoning trend. And when I am chosen, there is great public interest and scrutiny of my work, primarily because what I do in such cases is so at odds with American tradition. Of course, once policy makers decide to create a compensation program, it should work effectively and successfully. When this happens, the program should be a sound and innovative public policy initiative that accomplishes its goals.

But, ironically, this very success constitutes a challenge to the conventional, traditional, familiar methods of paying the American people. If it worked after 9/11, or the BP oil spill, why not try something similar the next time, or the time after that? This argument quickly takes hold—that we should make such special compensation the rule rather than the exception.

Some critics maintain that our existing tort system over-deters, distorts the professional judgments of often-sued individuals, such as physicians, is too inefficient and costly, or is not well adapted to the pursuit of justice. Gadflies deploy these arguments and more in support of the cause of tort reform. To some, the 9/11 fund and GCCF might appear to be perfect examples of a better way. These compensation programs could be viewed as precedents for broader, more comprehensive and pervasive tort reform affecting all of our federal, state, and local courts.

I disagree. I continue to believe that the American legal system, with its emphasis on judges, juries, and lawyers all participating in adversarial give-and-take, works well in the great majority of cases. Tort law is no exception. Critics can always list distressing individual cases that outrage our common sense, especially in complex mass toxic tort litigation. But these examples are few indeed when compared to the thousands of trials and verdicts that are handled fairly and equitably every day in courtrooms throughout our nation.

The case has not been made for wholesale replacement of the existing tort system. Piecemeal reform aimed at specific flaws in the system—limiting multiple punitive damage awards in the same litigation, enforcing more consistency in compensating for pain and suffering, providing administrative alternatives to deal with medical malpractice claims—is worthy of consideration, and model programs might be implemented to test the merit of such proposals. But radical changes—modifying the burden of proof at trial, federalizing state tort laws, adopting the "English rule," which requires the losing party in a tort lawsuit to pay the legal fees of the successful adversary—are unwarranted.

Rather than viewing the 9/11 fund and the GCCF as models for a new system to replace the traditional tort system, we should think of them as "safety valves," rare alternatives to the tort system implemented by policy makers when they conclude that tort litigation as usual will not do.

What these rare compensation programs do highlight is how government can respond effectively and efficiently to national trauma resulting from tragedy. And despite the differences in the circumstances giving rise to each program, there are elements common to all of them.

First and foremost is the necessity of political consensus and bipartisan support in creating a special pay program for special people. Without this consensus, no credible compensation program can be implemented. Political support from policy makers is essential, whether that support comes from the courts, the legislature, the executive, or a combination of all three. Such a broad consensus is—quite appropriately—difficult to achieve. It is reserved for the rarest of public tragedies, when national trauma compels an immediate unique response. The communitarian ethic I learned during my youth in Brockton must again emerge after a unifying, clarifying event. The 9/11 fund, the GCCF, and the corporate bailouts are perfect examples. The public demanded action and these compensation programs were the result. Not so the 1995 Oklahoma City bombing or the 2005 Hurricane Katrina tragedy. Homegrown terrorism or a natural disaster did not translate into special compensation. When the political tipping point is reached, the government acts.

A second common characteristic: more often than not, these pay programs are created on a track parallel to traditional dispute resolution procedures. They are rarely part of the court system (Agent Orange is an exception because of Judge Jack Weinstein's skill and creativity). Instead they are established as stand-alone entities, with only a tangential relationship to the other branches of government. Witness the relative independence of the 9/11 fund, the GCCF, and the Hokie Spirit Memorial Fund. Even Secretary Timothy Geithner and the Department of the Treasury decided to establish a special master for TARP executive compensation sep-

arate from the regular bureaucracy. All of these programs float in
a type of limbo land without firm political traction affixed to the
various branches of government. This can be both a blessing and
a curse.

Their uniqueness notwithstanding, the programs must be well
funded. In all of these special compensation programs, money has
been readily available to pay claims or determine executive compensation. Whether the source of the funds is a lawsuit settlement
(Agent Orange), public taxpayer money (the 9/11 fund), or private contributions (the Hokie Spirit Memorial Fund, the GCCF,
and private corporate pay), the money is *available now*, ready to
be dispensed without protracted argument and debate.

Efficient and speedy individual compensation determinations
will be made through an administrative system that will bypass
conventional legal proceedings. Procedural niceties, lawyer advocacy, and courtroom due process yield to the necessities of the moment—getting pay out the door to thousands of eligible claimants
with a minimum of fuss and bother.

Finally, when compensation determinations are not over-
whelmed by sheer volume (as with the GCCF), the programs are
dramatically improved if each individual is offered the right to be
heard, to express a personal opinion in a formal proceeding. This
opportunity for face-to-face discussion undercuts the natural perception of assembly-line justice, of claimants merely being cogs in
some mysterious bureaucratic machine. The right to be heard gives
each participant a personal stake in the outcome, a sense of involvement in the decision-making process. It enhances the credibility of any pay program and reminds recipients of the democratic
basis of the compensation effort.

After all, democratic, populist roots are at the core of these programs. Whether it is immediate cash in the wake of a national man-made calamity, or a compensation program traceable to populist anger over business excesses, these programs are established only because the public, acting through its elected representatives and agents, cries out for some type of government response. Not tomorrow, but today. Procedural niceties will follow later, along with an after-the-fact debate about the wisdom of delegating such awesome responsibility to one person. But for now, get the money out, fix corporate pay, and respond immediately and effectively to the crisis.

The public understands this. Citizen approval provides instant legitimacy to the effort. Millions of Americans personally unaffected by the tragedy acknowledge: "There but for fortune. I was not at the World Trade Center, or on the Virginia Tech campus, or in the Gulf of Mexico. I do not work on Wall Street. I am one of the lucky ones." These compensation programs are born out of this type of collective citizen sentiment.

If a pay program works as expected, it eventually secures the grudging admiration of claimants themselves. This approval does not come easy. It occurs over time. Immediate anger and frustration are natural during the first few months of administering these programs. Emotion rules. But as the money flows, as fair decisions emerge one by one, as time goes by, there is a chameleon-like transformation of attitude, an understanding that I am not the enemy, that I am simply implementing public policy to the best of my ability.

I constantly remind individuals affected by these payment programs to channel their anger and frustration at policy makers, not at me. As an administrator, I simply do what I am told—relying upon statutes, agency regulations, court orders, escrow agreements, or other enabling directives. The law establishes my jurisdiction. And I follow the law.

I have been selected to design and administer these unique initiatives because of my prior experience and effectiveness. Past success breeds repeat performances. This is the source of my credibility: meeting past challenges in deciding who gets what. But I assure anybody who will listen that I am only as effective and credible as my current assignment. One false move, one massive error, one failure—I am yesterday's news. My hold on credibility is tentative and fragile. Claimant attitudes reflect the current, the present, the immediate: "What have you done for me lately?" quickly undercuts any reliance on what I did yesterday. Today is all that matters.

What is important are the personality and character traits needed to stand up to the criticism and stress, and to labor effectively in a very emotional vineyard—empathy and sensitivity to the plight of those singled out for special consideration; confidence and firmness toward the critics. I turn the other cheek when face-to-face with a distraught victim or a businessman challenging my pay decisions. Life's unfairness is usually the real source of their anger. The nature of the compensation received is secondary.

But a strategic retreat is not an option when critics attack. Self-confidence and firmness then become virtues. You cannot allow yourself to be bullied when you are trying to administer a complex policy experiment. The public is usually supportive, appreciative of the difficulty of the task.

I point with pride to an interesting fact about my service over the past decades: the invective directed at me has sometimes been caustic and personal, but I have never been labeled as incompetent. I usually am accused either of being insensitive and lacking compassion for victims, or of being "too smart," "too clever by half" in pursuing some hidden agenda. I can defend myself against these charges. But I've never had to defend the diligence of my efforts or the seriousness with which I take the challenges of my work—because, I think, the facts speak for themselves.

And when my work is finished and I return to the private practice of law, there is always a fleeting hope that the compensation assignment just completed will be my last, the concluding chapter of a most interesting and challenging career as a special master and administrator. But it does not happen. In just the past few months—even while laboring on in administering the GCCF—I've again received requests to assist those in need.

The telephone rings: It's Governor Mitch Daniels and Attorney General Greg Zoeller of Indiana, asking me to help design and administer a compensation program to aid the victims of the Indiana State Fair Pavilion windstorm that left seven dead and scores physically injured. I immediately travel to Indianapolis to consult with state officials.

Another day, another call: It's Governor Dannel Malloy of Connecticut. A freak winter storm has left hundreds of thousands of Connecticut residents without power. The utility company is prepared to offer financial aid to all eligible residents. But who should be eligible, based on what criteria? Should the compensation be in the form of an invoice credit or actual cash? Neither the utility nor the governor is comfortable with designing the system. Will I help? I agree to give it a try. (It will be a credit, not cash.)

Still another afternoon, and my phone is ringing again: It's an official from Penn State University, embroiled in one of the most shocking cases of alleged child sexual abuse we've seen in decades. Merely as an option, the university is considering establishing some type of compensation program for the alleged victims. How much would such a program cost? Who would be eligible? What proof of harm would be required? What are the pros and cons? I grab a yellow legal pad and begin to outline ideas.

Assisting my fellow Americans in these efforts is one way I perform the role of responsible citizen. Getting caught in the crosshairs of criticism, resentment, and misunderstanding is a natural part of the work. You rally the troops and brace yourself for the onslaught. You move forward, implementing compensation directives. Your personal resolve is reinforced by the knowledge that you have been selected to do the job—and you are in the right.

And you know in your heart of hearts that it will not be your last assignment. Life guarantees misfortune.

APPENDIX

The following statistics provide important and pertinent data about the various compensation programs that I have designed, implemented, and administered over the past twenty-eight years. These statistics help the reader better understand the nature of the various compensation programs and their impact on the families of deceased victims, those physically injured, citizens of the Gulf region that suffered economic harm as a result of the oil spill, and corporate executives receiving compensation. The following data is also of interest to the American people who bear witness to these various, unique programs. This appendix also includes an organizational chart of the GCCF, evidence of the complexities associated with processing over 1 million Gulf oil spill claims.

AGENT ORANGE PAYMENT PROGRAM

- Total funds supplied by chemical companies: $243,375,926
- Allocated to Agent Orange Veteran Payment Program
  (i.e. damages paid to individual American victims):
  $172,775,853

- Paid to class action members in Australia and New Zealand: $5,000,000
- Allocated to Agent Orange Class Assistance Program: $42,000,000
- Paid to plaintiffs' attorneys: $13,825,000
- Retained for the Indemnity Fund in case of future litigation: $10,000,000

FEDERAL SEPTEMBER 11TH VICTIM COMPENSATION FUND OF 2001

- Total funds awarded: $7,049,415,536.64
- Number of awards to deceased victims: 2,880
- Average payment for deceased victims (tax free): $2,082,035.07
- Number of awards to physical injury victims: 2,680
- Average payment for injured victims: $392,968.11

HOKIE SPIRIT MEMORIAL FUND

- Total funds awarded from private donations: $7,074,377
- Number of awards for deceased victims: 32
- Payment per deceased victim: $208,000
- Number of awards for physical injury victims and those present at the site of the shooting: 48
- Average payment for physical injury victims and those present at the site of the shooting: $35,668.75

TARP EXECUTIVE COMPENSATION

Affected individuals included the top twenty-five highest paid executives at each of the following companies in receipt of TARP funds: American International Group, Inc.; Bank of America Corporation; Chrysler Group LLC; Chrysler Financial; Citigroup, Inc.; General Motors Company; and GMAC Financial Services.

- Highest post–TARP direct compensation for 2009 (included total cash salary, stock salary, and long-term restricted stock): $10.5 million
- Lowest post–TARP compensation for 2009: $100,000
- Average post–TARP compensation for 2009 (excluding top twenty-five employees whose compensation package did not include a base cash salary): approximately $2.5 million
- Average percent change between 2008 (pre–TARP) and 2009 (post–TARP) direct compensation: –47.9%

THE GULF COAST CLAIMS FACILITY: OVERALL STATISTICS (AS OF MARCH 9, 2012)

- Funds reserved: $20,000,000,000
- Funds distributed: $6,139,000,000
- Total claimants: 574,881
- Total emergency advance claimants: 169,203
- Total quick pay final claimants: 128,172
- Total interim claimants: 35,261
- Total full review final claimants: 67,143
- Total claimants denied or filing a deficient claim: 420,430

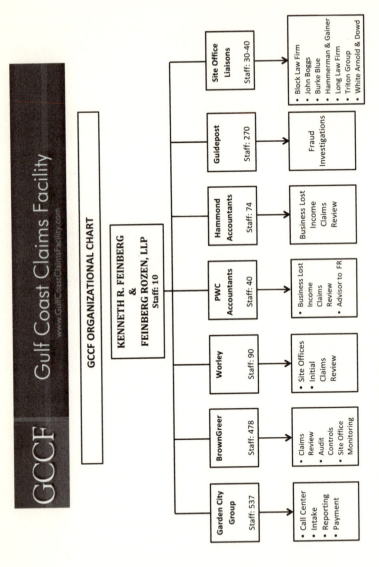

GCCF

Gulf Coast Claims Facility

www.GulfCoastClaimsFacility.com

GCCF ORGANIZATIONAL CHART

KENNETH R. FEINBERG
&
FEINBERG ROZEN, LLP
Staff: 10

Garden City Group
Staff: 537
- Call Center
- Intake
- Reporting
- Payment

BrownGreer
Staff: 478
- Claims Review
- Audit Controls
- Site Office Monitoring

Worley
Staff: 90
- Site Offices
- Initial Claims Review

PWC Accountants
Staff: 40
- Business Lost Income Claims Review
- Advisor to FR

Hammond Accountants
Staff: 74
- Business Lost Income Claims Review

Guidepost
Staff: 270
- Fraud Investigations

Site Office Liaisons
Staff: 30-40
- Block Law Firm
- John Boggs
- Burke Blue
- Hammerman & Gainer
- Long Law Firm
- Triton Group
- White Arnold & Dowd

Note: Citibank – Banking Institution used by GCCF

INDEX

Kenneth R. Feinberg, one of the nation's leading lawyers, has been front and center in some of the most complex public legal disputes of the past three decades: Agent Orange, asbestos, the closing of the Shoreham Nuclear Plant, the September 11th Victim Compensation Fund, and most recently the Gulf oil spill. A former prosecutor, chief of staff to Senator Edward M. Kennedy, and member of two presidential commissions, he is also adjunct professor of law at Georgetown University, the University of Pennsylvania, Columbia University, and New York University.

PublicAffairs is a publishing house founded in 1997. It is a tribute to the standards, values, and flair of three persons who have served as mentors to countless reporters, writers, editors, and book people of all kinds, including me.

I. F. STONE, proprietor of *I. F. Stone's Weekly*, combined a commitment to the First Amendment with entrepreneurial zeal and reporting skill and became one of the great independent journalists in American history. At the age of eighty, Izzy published *The Trial of Socrates*, which was a national bestseller. He wrote the book after he taught himself ancient Greek.

BENJAMIN C. BRADLEE was for nearly thirty years the charismatic editorial leader of *The Washington Post*. It was Ben who gave the *Post* the range and courage to pursue such historic issues as Watergate. He supported his reporters with a tenacity that made them fearless and it is no accident that so many became authors of influential, best-selling books.

ROBERT L. BERNSTEIN, the chief executive of Random House for more than a quarter century, guided one of the nation's premier publishing houses. Bob was personally responsible for many books of political dissent and argument that challenged tyranny around the globe. He is also the founder and longtime chair of Human Rights Watch, one of the most respected human rights organizations in the world.

·   ·   ·

For fifty years, the banner of Public Affairs Press was carried by its owner Morris B. Schnapper, who published Gandhi, Nasser, Toynbee, Truman, and about 1,500 other authors. In 1983, Schnapper was described by *The Washington Post* as "a redoubtable gadfly." His legacy will endure in the books to come.

Peter Osnos, *Founder and Editor-at-Large*